Secrets from the NATO Kitchens

Barbara Brandenburg (ed.)

Secrets from the NATO Kitchens

28 culinary adventures

Bibliografische Information der Deutschen Nationalbibliothek:
Die Deutsche Nationalbibliothek verzeichnet diese Publikation in der
Deutschen Nationalbibliografie; detaillierte bibliografische Daten
sind im Internet über http://dnb.d-nb.de abrufbar.

© 2009

Herstellung und Verlag: Books on Demand GmbH, Norderstedt

ISBN: 9783837098433

I wish to thank all the spouses who made this book possible
by providing recipes and/or other contributions.

My special thanks go to
the Language Services Section at the German Delegation to NATO
for proofreading and lending generous linguistic support.

TABLE OF CONTENTS

Foreword (p. 11)
Editor's note (p. 13)

Albania (p. 17)
Belgium (p. 23)
Bulgaria (p. 31)
Canada (p. 39)
Croatia (p. 45)
Czech Republic (p. 49)
Denmark (p. 59)
Estonia (p. 67)
France (p. 75)
Germany (p. 83)
Greece (p. 91)
Hungary (p. 101)
Iceland (p. 111)
Italy (p. 119)
Latvia (p. 133)
Lithuania (p. 141)
Luxembourg (p. 149)
The Netherlands (p. 153)
Norway (p. 159)
Poland (p. 165)
Portugal (p. 173)
Romania (p. 181)

Slovakia (p. 187)
Slovenia (p. 195)
Spain (p. 207)
Turkey (p. 215)
United Kingdom (p. 219)
United States of America (p. 225)

This and That (p. 233)

Last but not least (p. 261)

Index of all recipes in alphabetical order (p. 267)

Measures (p. 275)
Abbreviatons (p. 276)

FOREWORD

provided by Mrs Jeannine de Hoop Scheffer-van Oorschot, spouse of the Secretary General of the North Atlantic Treaty Organization

DIVERSE BUT UNITED

When you enter NATO HQ through the main entrance, you immediately come across the Cour d'Honneur with all the flags of the 28 NATO countries proudly flying in the gentle Brussels breeze. All the flags are different, yet they share many similarities in colour and design.

As soon as you step into the main building, you hear the buzz of the people working at NATO HQ and the numerous languages that are spoken by the NATO staff, the representatives of the 28 NATO member nations, their partner countries and the many foreign visitors.

It is always interesting to see and experience how people seemingly so diverse can also be so united. In NATO, it is common values and principles, and the mutual interest in guaranteeing peace and promoting stability and security that bind all these people together in a tight-knit community: a community that includes not just all the people working at NATO HQ, but also the family members that accompany them to Belgium.

But it is not only the flags and languages that are different in NATO; there is also a tremendous culinary diversity, and I would like to congratulate Barbara Brandenburg, spouse of the German Ambassador to NATO, for taking the initiative and compiling this collection of recipes from the spouses of the 28 Ambassadors to NATO. And of course, I should also like to thank the spouses themselves for having offered us a glimpse into their national kitchens and for sharing with us their typical national dishes.

May I also take this opportunity to promote another valuable activity at NATO: the NATO Wives Bazaar which recently celebrated its 40th anniversary. Its objective is to foster friendship between men and women of the international community in NATO by working together to raise money for charitable institutions, and the proceeds from this book will also go to charity. This is another good example of the 'esprit de famille' of the NATO community.

In the year of NATO's 60th birthday, perhaps I should have offered a recipe for a birthday cake! But even without the cake I am sure all of you will find something in here to your taste. I wish you all a most enjoyable read and many happy hours in the kitchen.

Jeannine de Hoop Scheffer – van Oorschot

EDITOR'S NOTE

Of course, it is not a new idea to publish a NATO cookbook. Several have already been published, the last one in 2004 with the title „Culinary Cosmic Top Secrets". But not only times and people change, there is also another very good reason to publish this one: in April this year, we celebrated 60 years of NATO and welcomed two new members to the Alliance.

Our national food represents where we come from and who we are: you may find thick and heavy dishes from cold countries, light and summery ones from those with a lot of sun, soups to share with a crowd of people, small expensive courses to have only with a handful of very good friends. There are also similar meals from different places of the world that still do not taste entirely the same. We represent our countries in serving dishes from our hometowns at official dinner tables and share the spirit of family life in providing native wines to accompany them. We distribute our culture, history and national objects of interest, but there is nothing like a good meal to start a conversation or even a dinner speech. As "trailing spouses" we follow our husbands through the whole world and always find it comforting when we are so lucky to discover the right ingredients on a market that allow us to cook a meal we used to prepare at home – in a place where we might feel lonely, abandoned and foreign.

To get into the mood we started with a cooking session among ourselves. During the work for the book, I have always been guided by the spirit of this evening: by reading the contributions of the NATO countries I learned a lot about them, and could not resist trying several of the recipes right away. Some were provided with pictures. In the end I opted for not publishing these because of unclear copyright issues. Nevertheless, when you read the descriptions they are so graphic you just have to close your eyes to imagine.

Although I squeezed the recipes into a certain format during the procedure of putting everything together, I opted for not modifying the text and style of the articles, to maintain NATO diversity.

As I am writing this, our project is almost finished and I can hardly wait to try the rest of the described meals.

Bon appétit - and of course: any profit from selling this book will be donated for charity purposes.

Barbara Brandenburg   Brussels, May 2009

RECIPES

ALBANIA

Recipes contributed by Mrs Ermira Kuko Samara, spouse of the Albanian Permanent Representative on the North Atlantic Council

'Anytime Soup'

***

Spinach Pies

***

Lamb Meat with Yogurt

***

Honey Cake

'ANYTIME SOUP'

INGREDIENTS:
2 midsized potatoes
5 midsized carrots
1 egg
1 tsp of starch
1/2 kg of natural full yogurt (not sour)
50 g of butter
1 litre of chicken or veal bouillon
parsley, salt and black pepper

PREPARATION:
Peel the carrots and potatoes. Wash them up and chop them into pieces. Boil the pieces of carrots and potatoes with 1 litre of bouillon until they get soft. Mix with a blender until it becomes a homogeneous mixture. In another pot mix the egg and starch in the yogurt. Put this mixture together with carrots and potatoes and let them boil, stirring for 5 minutes.

In the end, add chopped parsley, butter, salt and pepper.

Serve warm with spinach pies or toasted bread.

SPINACH PIES

INGREDIENTS:
1 package of ready-made rolled dough (pâte feuillettée)
200 g of spinach
100 g of feta cheese
100 g of Kaçkavall (or Caciocavallo) cheese
1 egg
40 g of butter
fennel, salt and pepper

PREPARATION:
Mix the slightly boiled spinach with the egg, cheese, fennel and butter. Cut the ready-made rolled dough in triangular forms, then fill them with the mixture.

Fold them in triangular forms and paint them with some (melted) butter. Bake in 200 °C oven for 20-25 minutes.

The soup is more common in the south of the country. The pies are a tradition in south-east Albania.

LAMB MEAT WITH YOGHURT

INGREDIENTS:
4 portions of pavé lamb meat (altogether approx. 500 g)
800 g of yoghurt
2 tbsp of rice
3 eggs
40 g of butter
3 tbsp of flour
fennel, salt and black pepper
leaves of laurel

PREPARATION:
Fry 4 portions of meat, salted and peppered together with leaves of laurel with a bit of butter in a pan (not on strong heat). Turn them 2-3 times, until properly fried. Add in the pan two spoons of rice and 200 ml of water. Leave them together with the meat until the water has evaporated.

In another bowl stir the yoghurt, eggs, flour, and chopped fennel. Take 4 small baking pans, put in each of them a piece of meat with part of the cooked rice and add in each of them the prepared mixture, proportionally divided. Pour some melted butter over them.

Bake in preheated oven and cook at 200 °C for 40 minutes.
Serve warm accompanied with green salad or any season salad.

This is a traditional meal in central Albania.

HONEY CAKE

INGREDIENTS:
200 g of flour
100 g of sugar
5 tbsp with honey
1 egg
1/2 tsp of baking soda
100 g butter
100 g walnuts

Syrup (boil for 5 minutes):
250 ml water
200 g sugar
10 g vanilla

PREPARATION:
Mix melted butter, sugar, egg, honey, and walnuts. Then add the flour and the baking soda. After mixing all the ingredients well, put the contents in the baking pan, whose bottom has been painted with a bit of butter and level it well.

Bake in preheated oven at 180 °C for 20-25 minutes.

Take the cake out of the oven, and after it cools down a bit, pour the lukewarm syrup over it uniformly.

Serve with strawberries and ice cream.

This is a typical dessert from the north-east part of the country.

BELGIUM

Recipes contributed by Mrs Chris Deroover,
spouse of the Belgian Permanent Representative on
the North Atlantic Council

Cream of White Asparagus Soup

***

Waterzooi of Fish

***

Chocolate Mousse

CREAM OF WHITE ASPARAGUS SOUP (4-6 SERVINGS)

INGREDIENTS:
1 1/2 pounds white asparagus
6 tbsp unsalted butter
6 cups chicken broth
2 cups boiling salted water
3 tbsp flour
salt, freshly ground white pepper to taste
1/2 cup whipping cream
1 large egg yolk
2 tbsp finely minced fresh chervil, a few chervil leaves for garnish

PREPARATION:
Peel the asparagus stalks with a sharp vegetable peeler. Break off the tips and reserve them. Cut the stalks into 1-inch pieces.

Melt 4 tbsp of the butter in a large saucepan over medium heat. Add the asparagus stalks and cook, stirring frequently, for 5 minutes. Add 2 cups of the chicken broth and simmer, covered, for 20 minutes.

Remove from the heat and let cool a little. Purée in a blender or food processor and set aside.

Cook the asparagus tips in the boiling saltwater until just tender, 2 to 3 minutes. Drain, refresh the asparagus tips under cold running water and reserve.

Melt the remaining 2 tbsp butter in a large saucepan over medium heat. Sprinkle the flour over the melted butter and stir with a wooden spoon until smooth. With a wire whisk gradually stir in the remaining 4 cups of chicken broth. Bring to a boil, stir once more and remove from the heat.

Stir the asparagus purée into the soup base. Season to taste with salt and pepper.

To serve the soup, whisk together the cream and egg yolk. Gently reheat the soup and stir in the cream mixture and the chervil. (Do not let the soup come to a boil or it will curdle!) Add the asparagus tips, heat through gently and serve.

Garnish each soup plate with a few chervil leaves.

WATERZOOI OF FISH (4 SERVINGS)

INGREDIENTS:
3 tbsp unsalted butter
4 leeks (only the white parts)
2 shallots
2 carrots
1/2 celery root
4 cups fish broth
1 cup dry white wine
1 tbsp fresh or 1 tsp dried thyme
1 bay leaf
a pinch of saffron threads
salt and freshly ground black pepper to taste
2 pounds fillet of firm-fleshed white fish (e.g. turbot, cod, monkfish, halibut)
1 1/2 cups whipped cream
3 large egg yolks
2 tbsp finely minced fresh parsley or chervil

PREPARATION:
Melt the butter in a large saucepan. Add the leeks, shallots, carrots and celery root (all sufficiently prepared and julienned) and cook, stirring frequently, until the vegetables have softened lightly but are not browned (about 5 minutes).

Pour in the fish broth and wine. Add the thyme, bay leaf and saffron. Simmer, covered, over medium heat for about 10 minutes. Season with salt and pepper.

Before serving, bring the broth and vegetables to a simmer over medium heat. Add the fish and poach, uncovered, in the simmering broth until just done (about 10 minutes). Remove the fish with a slotted spoon and keep warm.

Whisk the cream and egg yolks together, then gradually whisk in a ladleful of hot broth to temper the egg mixture. Slowly stir the egg mixture into the hot broth. Return the fish to the broth and reheat over very low heat (Do not allow it to come to a boil or the sauce will curdle!).

To serve, arrange the vegetables in the bottom of heated soup plates. Spoon the fish on top and ladle plenty of sauce over the fish and vegetables. Sprinkle with parsley and serve.

CHOCOLATE MOUSSE (4 SERVINGS)

INGREDIENTS:
5 oz bittersweet chocolate, chopped
1/4 cup brewed coffe
4 large egg whites (at room temperature)
2 tbsp confectioners' sugar
1/4 cup whipping cream (well chilled)
1 tsp dark rum, cognac or Grand Marnier (optional)

PREPARATION:
Place the chocolate and coffee in a Bain Marie and melt over lightly simmering water. Stir occasionally with a wooden spoon. Remove from the heat and let cool slightly.

Beat the egg whites until stiff. Gradually beat in the sugar and continue to beat until the egg whites hold stiff peaks. Do not overbeat to keep them from getting too dry.

In a separate bowl, beat the whipping cream.

Use a spatula to delicately fold the egg whites into the chocolate in three parts. Then carefully fold in the whipped cream and rum, cognac or Grand Marnier.

Spoon the chocolate mousse into 4 champagne flutes, wineglasses or ramekins. Cover tightly with plastic wrap and refrigerate for a few hours to let the mousse stiffen up.

Garnish with chocolate shavings or whipped cream.

BULGARIA

Recipes contributed by Mrs Mariana Ivanova,
spouse of the Bulgarian Permanent Representative on
the North Atlantic Council

Boiled Veal

***

Breaded Cheese Peppers

***

Chicken 'Thrace'

***

Milk Pie

BOILED VEAL

INGREDIENTS:
knuckles of veal
onion
carrots
celery
parsley roots
potatoes
canned tomatoes
parsley
horseradish
vinegar
salt, black pepper (well ground)

PREPARATION:
Clean and wash the veal knuckle. Cut the celery, the parsley roots, the onion and the carrots into big pieces. Fill a deep saucepan with cold water and put the meat in it. Leave the saucepan on the fire until it begins to boil. Remove the froth from the liquid (the bouillon must remain clear and transparent), add salt, black pepper and the vegetables that you've cut into big pieces. Leave the bouillon to boil at moderate temperature until the meat becomes soft and well-cooked and is easy to remove from the bones.

Remove the bones and the remnants from the vegetables (a part of the vegetables has dissolved in the bouillon giving it a particular peasant taste).Cut carrots, celery and potatoes into medium-size cubes and put them in another saucepan, in which you've poured salty boiling water beforehand. Cook these vegetables well but not too long – they must not lose their shape.

Cut the boiled meat into cubes, peel tomatoes and cut them into four equal pieces. Return the meat cubes to the bouillon. Add to the bouillon the cut and peeled tomatoes and the cooked vegetables. Leave the mixture to boil for a short while.

Grind the horseradish. Mix in a separate saucepan the ground horseradish, vinegar and salt until you obtain a pleasant taste to your liking.

The soup is served in a deep saucer. Distribute evenly the meat and the vegetables, pour the bouillon over them and sprinkle parsley that you've cut beforehand into fine pieces over each saucer.

REMARK:
Offer the mixture of vinegar, horseradish and salt to those who wish to add it to their soup.

BREADED CHEESE PEPPERS

INGREDIENTS:
baked peppers
cow's cheese
eggs
flour
bread crumbs
parsley
vegetable frying oil
green salad
salt, ground black pepper

PREPARATION:
Peel the baked peppers, remove their seeds and sprinkle them carefully with salt and black pepper. In order to prepare the stuffing mixture, use the following ingredients: cheese, parsley cut into small pieces, and eggs. Stuff the peppers, paying attention not to rip or tear them. Do not overstuff because the stuffing mixture may run out of the peppers while you fry them.

Before frying the stuffed peppers in heated vegetable oil, they have to be covered with bread crumbs. The mixture used for this is prepared with the following ingredients: flour, eggs and bread crumbs.

This is done as follows:

Roll the stuffed peppers in the flour, then roll them in the wellbeaten eggs and finally roll the peppers in the bread crumbs.

Fry the stuffed breaded peppers until they turn a golden colour. Take them out of the frying pan and arrange them on kitchen paper that will absorb the grease.

Before serving the peppers in a small dish with a diameter of 19 cm, sprinkle the bottom of the dish with the green salad cut into small pieces.

REMARK:
The oil in the frying pan has to be abundant (i.e. oil bath) so that the peppers will not stick to the bottom of the pan while you fry them.

CHICKEN 'THRACE'

INGREDIENTS:
chicken thigh steaks
yogurt
savory
garlic
vegetable oil
cow's butter
a slice of lemon
salt, ground black pepper
potatoes
dill

PREPARATION:
Remove the meat from the bone. Beat it carefully and evenly with a light wooden hammer. Cut into fine pieces or mince the garlic and the savory. Sprinkle the meat with the ground garlic and savory and leave the meat to soak in yogurt for 12 hours. Boil the potatoes (without peeling them) in slightly salty water. Be careful - the potatoes should not lose their shape. Do not over-boil the potatoes. Peel the boiled potatoes and cut them into big pieces, pour melted butter over them and sprinkle with finely cut dill.
Hang the meat for a while to let the yogurt ooze down from it. Roast the meat on a very hot grill, or fry it with a little vegetable oil in a frying pan that has ribs on the bottom. Grill/fry the meat until it becomes golden on both sides. Be careful – you should not allow the meat to stick to the bottom of the pan in which you fry it.
The meat is served in a dish with a diameter of 23 cm. Garnish the meat with the potatoes you have already prepared with the dill and a slice of lemon.

MILK PIE

INGREDIENTS:
fine sheets of pastry
milk
eggs
crystalline sugar
cow's butter
vanilla aroma

PREPARATION:
Heat the oven to 180 °C. Melt the butter. Put the fine sheets of pastry in a baking dish and pour the melted butter over them. Put the baking dish with the pastry sheets in the heated oven.
Bake until the pastry becomes light brown. Turn to bake the other side of the pastry if necessary.

Put the milk and the sugar in a deep pan and stir until the sugar dissolves completely, then add the vanilla aroma and the eggs to the mixture. Take the sheets of pastry from the oven and let them cool off for a while, after that break the pastry sheets into pieces and stir them.

Pour the mixture you have prepared (milk, sugar, eggs and vanilla aroma) over the pieces of broken pastry sheets and return the pastry into the oven. Bake at 200 °C until the pastry becomes golden brown.

Remove the pie from the oven and cut it into 7x7 cm squares. Serve the pie in a dish with a diameter of 19 cm.

CANADA

Recipes provided by Mrs Dorise Nina McRae,
spouse of the Canadian Permanent Representative on
the North Atlantic Council

Lobster Salad

***

Baked Ham with Maple Glaze

***

Sugar Pie with Whipped Cream

LOBSTER SALAD (6-8 SERVINGS)

INGREDIENTS:
3 (6-8 oz each) freshly boiled lobsters (shelled)
1 cup mayonnaise
2 small minced onions
6 hard boiled eggs (chopped)
1 cup sweet pickles (chopped)
1 tsp salt
pinch of pepper
looseleaf lettuce

PREPARATION:
Cut lobster into bite size pieces and toss with above ingredients.

Serve on lettuce leaves.

BAKED HAM WITH MAPLE GLAZE (6-8 SERVINGS)

INGREDIENTS:
1 (5 pound) fully-cooked, bone-in ham
1/4 cup maple syrup
1 tbsp bourbon
2 tbsp Dijon mustard
1 tbsp dry mustard

PREPARATION:
Preheat the oven to 325 °F (165 °C). Trim excess fat off the ham and score in a diamond pattern with a sharp knife,
making shallow cuts about inch apart. Place in a roasting pan.

Roast for 30 minutes in the preheated oven. In a small bowl, mix together the maple syrup, bourbon, Dijon mustard and dry mustard.

When the 30 minutes are up, brush 1/3 of the glaze over the ham. Bake 20 minutes, and repeat twice with remaining glaze.

Let the ham stand for 10 to 15 minutes before carving.

Serve with steamed vegetables.

SUGAR PIE WITH WHIPPED CREAM (6-8 SERVINGS)

INGREDIENTS for whipped cream:
1 cup heavy cream
1/4 cup sugar
1 tsp vanilla

PREPARATION:
Whip cream until almost stiff. Add sugar and vanilla; beat until cream holds peaks.

INGREDIENTS for sugar pie:
2 (26 oz.) cans evaporated milk
1/2 cup milk
2 cups granulated sugar
1/2 cup flour
ground cinnamon
ground nutmeg
butter
2 (8 inch) unbaked pie shells

PREPARATION:
Pour both milk and evaporated milk into pie shell. Mix sugar and flour thoroughly and sprinkle over milk. Stir with fingers to avoid scraping crust. Add several pats of butter and sprinkle with cinnamon and nutmeg.
Bake at 400 °F for 10 minutes, reduce heat to 350 °F and bake for another 30-35 minutes or until golden brown.

Serve slices topped with whipped cream.

CROATIA

Recipe found at: dalmatiankitchen.com

Rivica

***

RIVICA (CROATIAN STUFFED CALAMARI, 4 SERVINGS)

INGREDIENTS:
1 lb medium sized Calamari
¼ lb prosciutto
1 radicchio
3 cloves of garlic
2 tbsp parsley
freshly ground pepper
½ cup olive oil (or mixture of olive and sunflower oil)

PREPARATION:
Clean and wash the Calamari, and prepare the stuffing: finely chop the tentacles and prosciutto, then add raddichio (cut into thin, short strips), chopped parsley, and garlic. Season with ground pepper and mix well. Fill the Calamari with the stuffing, closing the open ends with toothpicks.

Arrange the Calamari in cold oil in a pan, cover, and slowly fry in the olive oil on both sides for 15-20 minutes.

Stuffed Calamari are best served with fried potato halves, or any kind of seasonal salad.

SUGGESTION:
to ease the filling process, the open ends of the Calamari can be widened by a small cut.

Preparation and cooking time: 35 minutes.

CZECH REPUBLIC

Recipes contributed by Mrs Hana Füleová, spouse of the Czech Permanent Representative on the North Atlantic Council

Ham Rolls with Horseradish Whipped Cream

***

Beef Soup with Liver Dumplings

***

Beef with Cream Sauce and Czech Raised Dumplings

***

Apples in Blankets

HAM ROLLS WITH HORSERADISH WHIPPED CREAM

INGREDIENTS:
200 g thin ham slices
0.2 l whipped cream
2 tbsp horseradish paste or grated horseradish
salt
1 tsp sugar
1 tsp lemon juice

PREPARATION:
Carefully stir horseradish, salt, sugar, and lemon juice into whipped cream, one by one.

Spread whipped cream on ham slices and roll firmly.

Put on plate; decorate with green salad and cherry tomatoes.

Serve cold with rolls or bread.

BEEF SOUP WITH LIVER DUMPLINGS

INGREDIENTS:
1.25 l beef broth (boullion cubes can also be used)
root vegetables: 1 carrot, 1 parsley root, 1 small celery root
100 g beef or veal liver
1 egg
20 g butter
2 cloves of garlic
1 small onion
5 tbsp breadcrumbs or 2 stale buns
salt
black pepper
dried marjoram
fresh parsley tips

PREPARATION:
Grind or cut up the liver, add salt, pepper, marjoram, melted butter, chopped onion and garlic, egg and breadcrumbs. Mix well.

Create small dumplings or gnocchi and cook in the beef broth.

Add chopped or shredded root vegetables and cook for 10 to 20 minutes.

Before serving, sprinkle with fresh chopped parsley.

BEEF WITH CREAM SAUCE

INGREDIENTS:
900 g sirloin of beef
150 g fat bacon
3 carrots, chopped or grated
3 parsnips, chopped or grated
1 small celery root, chopped or grated
2 onions, chopped
12 peppercorns
10 allspice grains
2 bay leaves
1/2 tsp dried thyme
salt, pepper
0.3 l sour cream
2 tbsp flour
preserved cranberries

PREPARATION:
Season meat with salt, pepper and thyme.

Fry bacon and onions in a large pan until brown.

Add the meat, and fry quickly on all sides.

Take meat out.

Add vegetables, and fry for a couple of minutes.

Put meat back, add water and stew until tender (approx. 1 hour), adding more water as necessary.

Take the cooked meat out.

Remove allspice grains and bay leaves, and puree vegetables.

Return vegetables to pot, add cream and flour (mixed together thoroughly), and simmer for at least 15 minutes.

Remove from heat, slice the meat, put on plate, and pour the sauce over the meat pieces.

Garnish with preserved cranberries, slices of lemon and whipped cream.

Serve with Czech raised dumplings.

CZECH RAISED DUMPLINGS

INGREDIENTS:
400 g flour (sifted)
1 package dry yeast
1 egg (beaten)
250-300 ml milk (lukewarm)
1 tsp salt
1/2 tsp sugar
2 rolls or 2-3 slices of bread cut into small cubes (better from the previous day)

PREPARATION:
Mix dry yeast, 100 ml of milk and sugar in small bowl.

Combine sifted flour, bread cubes and salt in large bowl.

Once yeast has dissolved and become bubbly, mix with flour mixture in large bowl.

Stir the mixture, adding remainder of milk and beaten egg.

Knead dough thoroughly into ball.

Place dough ball into bowl, cover with towel, and set in a warm place for an hour.

Dough should double in size during this time.

Separate dough into three pieces, knead again and form loaves.

Set loaves aside on plate and let rise for 1/2 hour (covered with towel).

Place loaves into a big pot of boiling salted water.

Cover and boil for 15-18 minutes. Make sure to slightly crack lid open to prevent the pot from boiling over.

Halfway through boiling, flip loaves over in boiling liquid so both sides are adequately cooked.

Remove from hot water and let cool on cutting board.

Cut dumplings with string or dental floss while still warm.

APPLES IN BLANKETS

INGREDIENTS:
puff pastry
4 apples (for example Granny Smith)
red currant jam
1 egg
sugar
chopped nuts

PREPARATION:
Peel apples and cut in half.

Remove cores and fill holes with jam.

Roll out puff pastry and cut into squares.

Wrap apple halves in pastry squares.

Brush with beaten egg and sprinkle with nuts.

Place on baking sheets.

Bake at 200 °C for approx 30 minutes until golden.

Sprinkle with sugar.

DENMARK

Recipes contributed by
Mrs Elisabeth Bloch Poulsen-Hansen,
spouse of the Danish Permanent Representative on
the North Atlantic Council

Hvidore Grilled Scallops

***

The Empress' New Year Cod

***

Summery Apple Parfait with Caramel Sauce

These recipees come from the kitchen at Hvidore Castle on the sea, a little to the north of Copenhagen.

This is where the dowager Empress of Russia, who was a Danish princess, spent her last years.

As the name indicates, beautiful little Hvidore is white and so is the menu.

HVIDORE GRILLED SCALLOPS
(4 SERVINGS)

INGREDIENTS:
12 scallops
250 g small (Danish) new potatoes
2 stems of dill
100 ml good olive oil
juice of 1 lime
salt and pepper

PREPARATION:
Boil the potatoes in lightly salted water with the dill stalks until just tender.

Fry the scallops on a grill pan for approx. 1-2 minutes on each side, according to size. Season with salt and pepper.

Coarsely chop the dill and mix with the olive oil and lime juice. Heat slighty.

When serving, place the potatoes on the plate with the scallops on top. Pour the dill olive oil over the dish. Decorate with sprigs of dill.

THE EMPRESS' NEW YEAR COD
(4 SERVINGS)

INGREDIENTS:
4 back pieces of cod, each 200 g
20 quail's eggs
100 g veal bacon
3 large beetroots
4 tbsp Dijon mustard
1½ tbsp white balsamico
1 tsp sugar
1 tbsp mustard seeds
oil for deep frying

PREPARATION:
Fillet the back of the cod and divide into 4 pieces. Turn in the olive oil and season with salt and pepper.

Place in an ovenproof dish and bake for about 8-10 minutes in the oven at 200C/390 °F. The cod should be placed skin side down.

Peel the beetroots and cut into very thin strips (julienne). Heat the oil and fry the beetroot julienne until crisp.

Poach the quail's eggs in boiling water with a little salt and vinegar for about 2 min.

Dice the bacon and fry until golden. Blanch the mustard seeds 3 times to remove the gelatine. Whisk white balsamico with sugar at a gentle heat. Season with salt and pepper and the lemon juice. Add the blanched mustard seeds and whisk with olive oil.

Arrange the cod on a large white plate with the deep-fried beetroot on top. Sprinkle the diced bacon round the fish and carefully place the poached eggs round the fish on the plate. Trail the oil and mustard emulsion round the fish with a spoon.

It is important that the plates have been warmed beforehand.

SUMMERY APPLE PARFAIT WITH CARAMEL SAUCE (8 SERVINGS)

INGREDIENTS:
500 g apples, e.g. Jona Gold (400 g when cored and peeled)
150 ml organic apple juice
1 tbsp lemon juice
2 tbsp sugar
4 pasteurised egg yolks
4 tbsp sugar
400 ml double cream
½ tsp vanilla seeds
1 stick cinnamon

PREPARATION:
Place the cored and peeled apples in a saucepan with the apple juice, lemon juice and cinnamon stick. Steam covered until almost soft. Remove the lid and stir the apples until they have the consistency of thick porridge. Flavour with sugar - the apple puree should be tangy.

Allow to cool completely and then remove the cinnamon stick.

Whisk the egg yolks, sugar and vanilla seeds until the sugar has dissolved. Whisk the cream and fold the cold apple puree into it. Now fold in the egg toddy. Pour into a mould. Cover. Freeze the parfait.

INGREDIENTS for Caramel Sauce:
200 g granulated sugar
lemon juice
4 tbsp water

PREPARATION:
Place the sugar in a saucepan, heat and allow to melt while stirring. Avoid getting sugar on the sides of the pan. Add about 10 drops of lemon juice. When the sugar begins to boil vigorously, do not stir it any longer, otherwise it will go lumpy. The heat must not be too strong, or the sugar will burn during the boilng process. Pour 4 spoonfuls of water into a glass and pour it onto the sugar in two halves, as soon as it has begun to colour. Mind your hands as the sugar can splutter. Stir, making sure that everything has melted. The mixture should be extremely runny, otherwise it will harden when cooled.

Take the parfait out of the mould and serve with the caramel sauce. Can be served with a crumble but tastes delicious on its own.

ESTONIA

Recipes provided by Mrs Ruth Lausma Luik,
spouse of the Estonian Permanent Representative on
the North Atlantic Council

Grilled Baltic Herring on a Bed of Salad

***

Minced Pork Wrapped in Cabbage Leaves

***

Raspberry Charlotte with Raspberry Sauce

L'Estonie, se trouvant au Nord de l'Europe et ayant quatre saisons bien marquées, offre de nombreuses sources d'inspiration aux amoureux de l'art culinaire, qui peuvent se réjouir des ingrédients saisonniers frais et savoureux.
Ce sont le mouton, le veau, le fromage de chèvre, le poireau sauvage, l'oseille fraîche et la perche, qui marquent les plats au printemps.

Avec l'arrivée de l'été florissant, vient le moment d'apprécier toutes les saveurs les plus sauvages et naturelles imaginables : des herbes, des baies du jardin et de la forêt, des chanterelles et des pommes de terre fraîches. Il ne faut pas oublier l'anguille et les écrevisses fraîches très populaires. Ils jouent tous le premier violon dans la symphonie estivale en Estonie.

Puis vient l'automne avec ses saveurs transformées en délices. C'est la saison des canneberges, des mûres, des noisettes et des salsifis noirs. Mais aussi de l'oie fermier et des poissons tels que la lamproie, le hareng, l'écale et la plie. Néanmoins, la meilleure partie de l'automne c'est la saison de chasse. La variété du gibier dans les forêts vierges et les îles littorales est impressionnante; on y trouve des faisans, des élans, du verrat et des chèvres sauvages.

Pendant l'hiver, quand les journées sont courtes et sombres, on se raffermit en mangeant de la viande fumée, de la choucroute, du boudin traditionnel de Noël, en buvant du vin chaud et en grignotant des pains d'épices.

Head isu ! Bon appétit !

GRILLED BALTIC HERRING ON A BED OF SALAD (6 SERVINGS)

INGREDIENTS:
30 whole Baltic herrings
1 pot salad
½ cucumber cut into strips
5 cl chopped dill
1 dl vinaigrette dressing

PREPARATION:
Clean the herring leaving the heads and tails on. Grill the fish on both sides on a salted cast-iron pan. Toss the salad ingredients in the vinaigrette dressing. Place a helping of salad on each plate and stack the Baltic herrings upright over it with their tails up.

Vinaigrette dressing: 5 cl olive oil, 1 tsp gourmet salt, ½ tbsp sugar, 1 tbsp white balsamic vinegar.

The Baltic herring may be substituted with sardines.

MINCED PORK WRAPPED IN CABBAGE LEAVES

INGREDIENTS:
1.5 kg white cabbage
water
salt
600 g minced pork
2 eggs
2 dl cream
75 g onion
100 g chopped cabbage
1 tbsp butter for sweating
150 g boiled pudding rice (5 cl uncooked rice = 150 g cooked)
50 ml dark treacle
1 tsp salt
1 tsp marjoram
freshly ground white pepper

PREPARATION:
Remove the stalk and boil the cabbage in salted water. Peel off the leaves as they become soft. You will need 16 medium size leaves for 6 portions. The heart of the cabbage can be chopped up, cooked and used in the filling.

Sweat the chopped remains of the cabbage and onion in the butter and let them cool. Add the meat, treacle, eggs, cream and rice and mix well. If necessary, thin the filling with cream. Fry a trial piece and taste for flavour. Add seasoning if necessary.

Use a knife to pare the thick stems of the cabbage leaves thinner.

Place a small pile of the filling on each of the leaves, fold them over into packages and place them side by side on a greased oven tray. Brush the surface of the rolls with melted butter and drizzle about 5 cl of treacle over them. Cook them in the oven at 200 °C until their surface takes on an attractive colour. Turn the rolls over during the cooking process. Add a little (2-3 dl) mild meat stock to the oven tray and continue cooking the rolls in the oven at 150 °C. When they are almost done, turn them over once again, pour 3 dl of cream over them and cook them till they are done.

Remove the rolls from the oven tray and use the cooking juices as a base for the sauce. Add about 1,5 dl of cream and thicken with cornflour if necessary. Taste for flavour and add seasoning if needed.

Serve the rolls with vegetables and mashed lingonberries.

RASPBERRY CHARLOTTE WITH RASPBERRY SAUCE (8-12 SERVINGS)

INGREDIENTS:
2 eggs
1 dl sugar
1 dl flour
½ tsp baking powder
raspberry jam

PREPARATION:
Cream the eggs and sugar into a froth, and add the mixed flour and baking powder. Spread the mixture onto an oven tray covered with baking paper and bake it at 170 C for 7-8 minutes. Cool. Spread a small layer of raspberry jam over the cake base and fold it into a roll about 4 cm in diameter.

INGREDIENTS for Raspberry Sauce:
700 g raspberries
1 dl sugar

PREPARATION:
Purée the raspberries in a blender. Strain the seeds out by pressing the purée through a fine sieve. This will produce 6 dl of juice, of which 3 dl is used for the pudding and 3 dl for the sauce.

INGREDIENTS for Raspberry Pudding:
5 egg whites
2 dl cream (35% fat)
3 dl raspberry sauce
1 dl sugar
3 dl whipped cream
5 gelatine sheets (225x70 mm)

PREPARATION:
Mix the cream, egg yolks and sugar together and cook in a bain-marie. Soak the gelatine sheets in cold water and add them to the hot mixture of cream, egg yolks and sugar to dissolve. Then add the raspberry sauce. When the mixture has cooled slightly, add the whipped cream.

Take a round mould or a bowl. Place the slices of cake side by side around the edge and pour the pudding mixture into the middle. Chill till set.

Turn the pudding out onto a glass serving plate, or slice and serve directly on individual plates. Garnish with raspberry sauce, whole raspberries and melissa leaves.

Recipes adapted from the book "Best Kitchen in Town"

FRANCE

Recipes provided by Mrs Carine Vinchon,
spouse of the French Military Representative on
the North Atlantic Council

Crevettes à l'Ail

***

Tajine d'Agneau aux Citrons Confits

***

Salade d'Oranges et Tuiles aux Amandes

MENU MÉDITERRANÉEN

As I grew up in the south of France, I have chosen a southern menu with a lot of sunny flavours.

CREVETTES À L'AIL

INGREDIENTS:
400 g large shrimp
4 garlic cloves
1 red pepper
1 large cup fresh parsley
6 tbsp olive oil
salt and pepper

PREPARATION:
Heat 4 tbsp of olive oil on the stove in a large pan.

Add the shrimps and cook 5 minutes on each side. Set aside in a dish.

Grind garlic, parsley and pepper. Put the mixture in the same pan with the rest of the olive oil. Cook without burning the garlic ...

Add the shrimp, salt and pepper.

Serve hot or warm on a salad bed.

TAJINE D'AGNEAU AUX CITRONS CONFITS (6 SERVINGS)

INGREDIENTS:
1.2 kg shoulder of lamb, cut in fragments
1 tbsp ground cumin, 1 tsp red pepper
1 piece (6 cm long) of fresh ginger
4 preserved lemons (in every Arab shop or see the recipe below)
200 g black olives or violet (not compulsory)
2 onions
2 garlic cloves
1 tbsp of olive oil
1 coriander bouquet
3 zucchinis

PREPARATION:
In a deep pan, on the stove, heat the spoon of olive oil; add the chopped onions and the crushed garlic cloves.

Add the fragments of lamb and let them bronze. Grate the fresh ginger. Blend in the meat, the cumin, the red pepper and the ginger. Mix well. Deglaze the pot with some water. The sauce must be plentiful. If not, add more water.

Let simmer on low fire, covered, for 90 minutes. In a flat cooking dish for the oven, cut zucchinis in rather thick slices, cover with the simmered meat and top with the lemons cut in half or in smaller pieces, olives and coriander.

Season to taste, do not add too much salt if you added olives.

Cover with aluminum foil and bake in the oven at 180 °C for 1 hour.

Serve with medium size couscous (300 g couscous and 35 cl water).

PREPARATION:
Pour the couscous into a salad bowl, add salt and olive oil. Bring the water to a boil, and pour it on the couscous. Let the mixture stand for 5 minutes. Fluff the couscous with a fork. You can prepare it way in advance and heat at the last minute, covered, in the microwave.

PRESERVED LEMONS

INGREDIENTS:
6-7 juicy, ripe lemons
extra lemons to make up juice
1 sterilized half litre jar
½ cup salt

PREPARATION:
Put one tbsp of the salt into the bottom of the jar. Cut crosses in the lemons to within the 1/2 inch of the bottom so that they are still joined as one. Sprinkle salt on the exposed flesh. Squoosh the lemons into the jar, packing down tightly as you go, adding more salt evenly between layers. If there is not enough juice expelled by the lemons, to cover them all sufficiently, then add more fresh lemon juice until they are all submerged. Seal the jar. Leave the jar at room temperature for 30 days, shaking the jar each day to distribute the juices throughout the jar. To use the lemons, first rinse them a little bit.

Store in refrigerator for up to 6 months.

NOTE:
You can add spices to the lemons for preserving - cloves, coriander seeds, peppercorns, cinnamon stick, bay leaf.

SALADE D'ORANGES ET TUILES AUX AMANDES

INGREDIENTS:
50 g soft unsalted butter
100 g sugar
1 big tbsp of flour
juice of half an orange
100 g sliced almonds

PREPARATION:
Preheat oven to 180 °C. In a bowl, mix sugar, butter, juice and flour. Carefully add the almonds.

Place small spots of dough on a well-buttered baking sheet (or parchment paper), spots rather distant from each other, they will run with the heat. Watch the cooking (a few minutes) and remove when they have obtained a golden color.

Let cool down.

PREPARATION Salade d'Oranges:
Peel 1 kg of oranges, taking off the orange and the white skins. Slice and arrange in a rather flat salad bowl.

Make a syrup with the juice of 6 mandarins, 2 tbsp of sugar, 1 tear of Grand Marnier. Reduce over a low fire.

When cold add some cinnamon and 1 big tbsp of orange blossom water. Pour over oranges and refrigerate.
Serve with a "tuile aux amandes"

GERMANY

Recipes provided by Mrs Barbara Brandenburg, spouse of the German Permanent Representative on the North Atlantic Council

Old German Potato Soup

***

Beef Olives

***

Semolina Pudding

OLD GERMAN POTATO SOUP

INGREDIENTS:
700 g floury boiling potatoes
50 – 75 g celeriac
250 g carrots
1 onion
1 bay leaf
1 clove
40 g (3 tbsp) butter
1.5 litres hot vegetable stock
200 g leeks
125 ml whipping cream or 150 g crème fraiche
Salt, freshly ground pepper, dried marjoram leaves, grated nutmeg
For the garnish:
200 g chanterelles
1 onion
25 g (2 tbsp) butter
2 tbsp chopped herbs, e.g. chervil, chives, flat-leaved parsley

PREPARATION:
To make the soup, wash the potatoes, peel and rinse. Peel the celeriac and cut out the bad parts. Peel the carrots, cut off the green leaves and tips. Wash the celeriac and carrots and leave to drain. Cut all these prepared vegetables into small cubes or dice. Peel the onion and stud it with the bay leaf and clove.

Melt the butter in a pan. Add the diced celeriac and carrots and brown lightly while stirring all the while. Now add the diced potatoes, studded onion and vegetable stock. Cover, bring to the boil and cook over medium heat for about 20 minutes.

Meanwhile, remove the outer leaves of the leeks, cut off the root ends and dark green leaves. Cut in half, wash thoroughly, leave to drain and slice. Add the sliced leeks to the soup, cover and cook for another 10 minutes.

Remove the onion, studded with the bay leaf and clove. Remove about one-third of the potato and vegetable mixture from the soup, purée, stir in the whipping cream and pour the puréed mixture back into the soup. Heat up the soup again and season with salt, pepper, majoram and nutmeg.

For the garnish clean the chanterelles with a brush and remove any bad parts. If necessary, use a special mushroom-brush, but do not wash or rinse the chanterelles. Peel the onion and dice finely. Melt the butter in a pan, add the diced onion and fry in the melted butter, stirring continuously. Add the chanterelles and fry for about 5 minutes, stirring frequently.

Add the onion-chanterelle mixture to the soup and simmer for about 5 minutes. Sprinkle with herbs just before serving.

If desired, small Vienna sausages may also be added to the soup.

BEEF OLIVES

INGREDIENTS:
4 slices beef topside, 180 – 200 g each
Salt, freshly ground pepper
Medium mustard
60 g streaky bacon
4 onions
2 medium sized pickled gherkins
1 bunch soup vegetables
2 tablespoons cooking oil (e.g. sunflower oil)
about 250 ml hot water or vegetable stock
20 g (3 tbsp) plain flour
2 tbsp water

PREPARATION:
Pat the slices of beef with kitchen paper, sprinkle with salt and pepper and spread with 2-3 tsp of mustard. Cut the bacon into strips. Peel 2 onions, halve and cut into slices. Cut the pickled gherkins into strips.

Put the prepared ingredients on the slices of meat. Roll up the slices lengthwise and tie with kitchen string or special metal sticks.

Peel and quarter the remaining 2 onions. Prepare the soup vegetables. Peel the celeriac and cut out any bad parts. Peel the carrots and cut off green leaves and tips. Wash the vegetables and let them drain. Remove the outer leaves of the leeks, cut off the root ends and dark green leaves. Cut in half lengthwise, wash thoroughly and leave to drain. Cut the prepared ingredients into small pieces.

Heat the oil in a saucepan or pan. Brown the beef olives well on all sides. Fry the onions and soup vegetables briefly, then add half the hot water or stock and the beef olives. Braise covered on medium heat for about 1 ½ hours.

While braising, turn the beef olives from time to time and periodically replace the evaporated liquid with hot water or stock. When the olives are cooked, remove the sticks or string, place on a preheated plate and keep warm.

Strain the cooking juices through a sieve, make up to 375 ml water or stock and bring to a boil. Mix the flour with water and stir into the cooking liquid with a whisk, taking care to prevent any lumps from forming. Bring the sauce to a boil and cook uncovered over low heat for about 5 minutes, stirring occasionally. Season the sauce to taste with salt, pepper, mustard.

Beef olives are usually accompanied by red cabbage and cooked potatoes.

SEMOLINA PUDDING

INGREDIENTS:
½ vanilla pod
500 ml milk
75 g sugar
grated peel of ½ untreated lemon
50 g soft wheat semolina flour
1 medium egg

PREPARATION:
Cut open the vanilla pod lengthwise and scoop out the flesh. Add sugar, lemon peel, vanilla pod and flesh to the milk in a pan and bring to the boil. Add the semolina, stirring continuously. Bring to the boil and cook for about 1 minute while stirring.

Take the pan from the heat and remove the vanilla pod. Separate the egg and stir the egg yolk into the milk and semolina mixture. Beat the egg white very stiff and fold carefully into the hot pudding.

Rinse the mould, bowl or ramekins in cold water and fill with the pudding. Leave to cool and then refrigerate for about 3 hours.

Carefully loosen the pudding around the edges and turn out onto a plate.

Serve the semolina pudding with fresh fruit, stewed plums, puréed apricots or red fruit pudding (for recipe, see in the This-and-That section at the end of this book).

GREECE

Recipes provided by Mrs Elizabeth Stamatopoulos, spouse of the Greek Permanent Representative on the North Atlantic Council

Garidas me Feta (Shrimp Baked with Feta)

***

Roast Lamb, Peas with Dill and Fresh Onions, Oven Baked Potatoes

***

Ravani

GARIDAS ME FETA (SHRIMP BAKED WITH FETA)

This recipe is one of my favourites for starters. It was given to me by an excellent cook. You should take into account that it is not on the light side, so be aware of what you will serve as a main course.

INGREDIENTS:
3 cups sweet ripe tomatoes, peel and remove seeds (you can use plum canned tomatoes according to season and availability)
600 g of shrimp, shelled and deveined (you should have at least 24 large shrimps)
1/4 cup of olive oil
1 tsp finely chopped garlic
1/4 cup fresh fish broth
1 tsp crushed dried oregano
1 tsp dried red pepper flakes
2 tbsp drained good quality capers
salt and freshly ground pepper
3 tbsp of butter
150 g of feta cheese
1/4 cup of ouzo, a Greek anise-flavoured liqueur

PREPARATION:
Preheat oven to 180 °C.

Put the tomatoes in a saucepan and cook until reduced to about 2 cups.

Heat the olive oil in another skillet and add the garlic, stirring. Add the tomatoes, and mix.

Add the fish broth, oregano, pepper flakes, capers and salt and pepper to taste.

Heat the butter in a skillet and add shrimp. Cook briefly, less than 1 minute, stirring and turning until they turn pink.

Spoon equal portions of half the sauce in 4 individual baking dishes and arrange 6 shrimp plus equal amounts of the butter in which they cooked in each dish. Spoon remaining sauce over the shrimp.

Crumble the cheese and scatter it over all. Place the dishes in the oven and bake for 10 to 15 minutes, or until bubbling hot.

Remove the dishes from the oven and sprinkle each dish with one tablespoon ouzo and ignite if desired. Serve immediately.

ROAST LAMB

As a main course I picked leg of lamb, peas with dill and fresh onions, and oven baked potatoes.

INGREDIENTS for Roast Lamb:
leg of Lamb (the weight depends on how many you want to feed)
salt and pepper
rosemary
olive oil

PREPARATION:
Place your leg of lamb on a roasting pan, and rub well with coarse salt, and pepper.

Cut little slits in the leg of lamb, and stuff with salt, pepper, and rosemary leaves.

Pour a little olive oil and randomly place some rosemary branches.

Bake at 170 °C. The time will vary according to weight and how well you want it cooked.

PEAS WITH DILL AND FRESH ONIONS

I really like this recipe ...

INGREDIENTS:
500 g of sweet small peas
1 small shallot, finely chopped
6 medium sized spring onions finely chopped (you chop both the white and green part)
3 tbsp of fresh dill, chopped
one glass of good dry white wine
salt and freshly ground pepper
olive oil, about 5 tbsp

PREPARATION:
In a heavy pot, sauté the spring onions and shallot in olive oil until wilted.

Add the dill and peas and keep stirring.

Add salt, freshly ground pepper and white wine, stir, add a little water and cover with lid. You can add a little water if liquid is absorbed.

Let simmer on low heat for about 20 to 30 minutes.

This is a dish you can prepare even a day in advance.

ROAST POTATOES, BAKED IN OLIVE OIL AND HERBS

INGREDIENTS:
potatoes
olive oil
garlic, cut very fine, or if you want, you can marinate the garlic in the olive oil for several hours; remove garlic and use the marinated oil.
fresh or dry oregano
fresh thyme
lemon juice
coarse salt and freshly ground pepper
a very small piece of butter

PREPARATION:
Slice and cut your potatoes.

Place in a glass baking dish.

Add all ingredients except the butter and mix thoroughly together with potatoes. Then dot the butter on the top.

Bake at 180 °C until soft.

You may want to keep turning the potatoes every once in a while so they all bake in the juice.

RAVANI

This dessert is a moist tasty cake made with semolina and flour. It is quite easy to make, if you follow the recipe as written.
Semolina you can find in Greek specialty shops, or else some of the supermarkets also carry it, i.e. 'Delhaize'.
I would like to bring to your attention that you can reduce the sugar if you find it too sweet; I often do that with other dessert recipes as well.

INGREDIENTS:
1 1/2 cups fine semolina
1 1/3 cups self rising flour
1 1/2 tsp baking powder
1 tsp vanilla
1/2 tsp salt
8 eggs
1 1/3 cups sugar
4 tbsp lukewarm milk

For the syrup you will need:
3 cups sugar
2 1/2 cups water
6 tbsp butter
2 tbsp lemon juice
1 1/2 tsp finely grated zest of lemon

PREPARATION:
Preheat oven to 175 °C. Grease a 30 cm rectangular cake tin.

In a bowl, add all dry ingredients: semolina, flour, baking powder, vanilla, and salt. Mix and put aside.

In a mixer bowl, beat eggs with sugar until creamy and light.

You then add the milk, one tablespoon at a time, mixing after each addition.

Stop the mixer and with a wooden spoon or spatula fold in dry ingredients one spoonful at a time in a slow circular motion. You must be careful because the egg mixture is very sensible.

Your dough should be light and fluffy. Pour in baking pan and put in preheated oven. Bake for 30 to 35 minutes.

For the syrup …
In a small pot, add sugar and water and let boil for 5 minutes on medium heat.

Add the butter, lemon juice and lemon zest to the sugar and water. Mix with wooden spoon until the butter melts and ingredients have blended well together. You will then remove the pot from the stove.

The cake should be baked and still warm, when you pour the hot syrup.

Pour syrup one spoonful at a time over the warm cake. Syrup should not be poured in one as your cake might drop.

Once completely cooled you can cut the cake into squares and place on your serving platter. You can garnish with a white almond over each piece.

Enjoy!

HUNGARY

Recipes contributed by Mrs Csilla Ferenczy,
spouse of the Hungarian Permanent Representative on
the North Atlantic Council

Eggs in Aspic 'Munkácsy Style'

***

Consommé with Tokay Wine

***

Fillet of Beef 'Budapest Style'

***

Sponge Cake 'Somló Style'

Hungarian cuisine and Hungarian hospitality have become inseparable notions. As early as in the 17th century Hungarian chefs have served throughout the royal courts of Europe and have contributed to the fame of Hungarian cuisine. Travellers, visitors, and, later on, hundreds of thousands of tourists have experienced the delights of traditional Hungarian food, and have carried the fame of unique dishes way beyond the borders of our country. Yet, the grand masters and innovators of Hungarian cuisine have always sought to break out of the straight-jacket of the famous "Goulash" and intended to blend Hungarian tradition with the most modern trends of international cuisine. This innovative and experimenting spirit has led to the emergence of such world famous brands as the Gundel restaurant in Budapest. And it is exactly this challenge that awaits any modern-day Hungarian chef in Brussels, one of the culinary capitals of Europe.

The wide variety of national culinary habits and traditions in NATO creates a fiercely competitive environment on the culinary front. The task of Mr Zsolt Farkas, the chef of the Hungarian NATO Mission, is therefore twofold – he needs to act as the trusted custodian of the best Hungarian culinary traditions and practices, and he needs to blend these traditions with the refined international taste and tradition of the multinational NATO community. I have always relied on his advice and innovative spirit, be it for a quick reception, an afternoon tea, or the most complex dinner party, and our guests have always been provided with a unique experience, yet, with an unmistakeably Hungarian flavour.

It is, therefore, my special pleasure to offer for your kind attention the following menu created by chef Farkas based on traditional Gundel-recipes.

EGGS IN ASPIC MUNKÁCSY STYLE

This tasty dish was named after the world famous Hungarian painter Mihály Munkácsy (1844-1900).

INGREDIENTS:
250 g cooked fish
200 g tomatoes
120 g mushrooms
200 g celeriac sauce remoulade
12 poached eggs
Tarragon
600 g fish aspic

PREPARATION:
Cook and cube the peeled tomatoes, mushrooms and celeriac. Flake the cooked fish. Mix the vegetable and fish with a small amount of melted aspic and sauce remoulade. Spread the fish salad on a round glass platter.

To prepare the sauce remoulade: using an egg yolk and 1 3/4 dl oil, prepare mayonnaise. Add to the mayonnaise: sweet cream, mustard, salt, black pepper, sugar, capers, anchovy paste, chives, tarragon leaves, and finally chopped gherkins. This will result in a piquant sauce. Chill the remoulade well.

Poach the eggs in salted water to which vinegar is added for 3 minutes. The yolk of the eggs should remain soft. Lift out the poached eggs carefully and firm the edges. Pour aspic into the bottom of 12 small moulds. Let the aspic set in the mould, then decorate each with tarragon leaves, place a poached egg on the top of the set aspic, fill the mould with lukewarm aspic and refrigerate the moulds.

Before serving unmould the eggs on the top of the fish salad platter by dipping the mould into hot water for a short time.

Decorate with aspic and lettuce leaves.

Suggested wine: Szeremley Badacsonyi Kéknyelü 2004

CONSOMMÉ WITH TOKAY WINE

INGREDIENTS:
600 g lean beef
1 egg white
20 g (4 tsp) tomato paste
600 g beef bones
300 g soup vegetables
60 g celeriac
25 g onion
30 g mushrooms
60 savoy cabbage
salt, pepper, ginger root, garlic

PREPARATION:
Grind the lean beef, mix it in a soup pot with egg white and tomato paste, add 2 l of cold water or stock. Add the bones, sliced soup greens, spices. Bring it to a boil, then simmer for 3 hours (do not remove the foam as the soup boils).

Let the soup settle, then pour it through a cheese cloth very carefully. If the soup has a lot of fat on the surface, take it off with a spoon.

Consommé can also be prepared from chicken or pheasant.

Just before serving add the Tokay wine to the boiling soup, 3-5 cl per person. Tokaji Aszú would give the most pronounced taste to this soup, but because it is sweet, it is suggested to use dry Tokay Szamodorni.

FILLET OF BEEF BUDAPEST STYLE

INGREDIENTS:
1 kg beef fillet, prepared mustard, oil, pepper
3 portions of boiled rice
60 g lard, 120 g onion
10 g paprika, 30 g tomato paste, salt
300 g veal or pork bones
150 g green peppers
150 g mushrooms
150 g goose liver
80 g smoked bacon, 30 g lard
150 g green peas, salt, 120 g lard

PREPARATION:
Use properly aged beef for this dish. Marinate 6 slices of the fillet in mustard, oil and pepper in the refrigerator for several days.

Prepare 3 portions of boiled rice. Meanwhile, lightly brown the chopped onion in lard, add the paprika and tomato paste and stir, then immediately add about 3 dl water, salt and the bones. Boil for half an hour to prepare a pörkölt sauce. Remove the bones and strain the sauce.

Cut the green peppers, mushrooms, goose liver and bacon into squares. Wilt the bacon in a small amount of lard, then add the rest of the cut ingredients and fry them together. Pour the pörkölt over the fried ingredients. Simmer to blend the flavours in the gravy. Cook the green peas in a small amount of salted water.

Just before serving, panfry the fillet steaks medium to medium rare, sprinkle salt over the fried fillet, place them on a bed of rice, pour the sauce over them, pour the drained green peas on top. Serve with deep-fried potatoes.

Suggested wine: Takler Merlot Szekszárd 2003

SPONGE CAKE SOMLÓ STYLE (10-12 SERVINGS)

This delectable dessert is the creation of Károly Gollerits, who was the Maître d'hotel of the Gundel Restaurant for 16 years.

INGREDIENTS:
For the topping:
100 g walnutS
80 g raisins
1 dl rum

For the sponge cake:
8 eggs
160 g flour
160 g sugar
40 g walnuts
20 g cocoa

For the vanilla cream:
4 egg yolks
30 g flour
100 g sugar
1/2 dl milk
1 vanilla bean

For the syrup:
200 g sugar
1/3 dl water
15 cl rum
lemon or orange peel

20 g cocoa
80 g raspberry or apricot jam
300 g sweet cream
3 portions (6 tbsp) chocolate syrup

PREPARATION:
Soak the raisins in the rum and grind the walnuts a day ahead of time. To prepare the sponge cake: beat the egg whites in a mixing bowl, slowly add the sugar, beat it until stiff, stir in the eggs yolks, then the flour. Divide the dough into 3 parts; into the first 1/3 mix in 40 g ground walnuts, into the second 1/3 mix in the cocoa, the third portion remains plain sponge cake. Bake the finger-thick cake layers in a steam-free medium hot oven.

For the vanilla cream: scald the milk with the vanilla bean, add the egg yolks, sugar and flour, and to be on the safe side, add a small amount of gelatine.

For the syrup: cook the sugar for 15 min. in the water, which is flavoured with the lemon and orange peel. When the syrup is cool, add the rum.

To assemble the cake, the bottom layer is the walnut flavoured sponge cake. Sprinkle with 1/3 of the syrup, spread 1/3 of the walnuts and raisins over it and 1/3 of the vanilla cream over the walnuts. The middle layer is the cocoa flavoured sponge cake, then repeat the filling process. The top is the plain sponge cake, which is sprinkled with rum, then the jam is spread over it before the vanilla cream is added. Sprinkle the top with cocoa.

Refrigerate the cake for a few hours.

Serving can be either by cutting the cake into squares and placing them on individual glass dishes or by scooping tablespoon size "dumplings" out of the cake. Top the cake with whipped cream and with thick cocoa syrup.

Suggested wine: Tokaji Aszú 5 puttonyos Hétszölö 2000

ICELAND

Recipes contributed by Mrs Hólmfridur Kofoed-Hansen, spouse of the Icelandic Permanent Representative on the North Atlantic Council

Panfried Fillet of Arctic Char on Fennel, Tomato and Orange

***

Braised Leg of Lamb with White Wine, Sage, Tomatoes and Mushrooms

***

Skyr Soufflé Ice Cream

PANFRIED FILLET OF ARCTIC CHAR ON FENNEL, TOMATO AND ORANGE
(4 SERVINGS)

INGREDIENTS:
4 fillets of Arctic Char (approx. 5 ounce each), cleaned for all bones and cut in 8 pieces
2–3 shallots, finely chopped
2–3 garlic gloves, finely chopped
½-1 fennel bulb (according to size)
4–6 tomatoes
2 oranges
1 fl oz fish or chicken stock
2-3 tbsp Icelandic butter
2 tbsp tarragon leaves, shredded
sea salt and white pepper to taste

PREPARATION:
Take the fennel bulb and remove the core and outer layer, if needed, and slice very fineley and thin.

With a sharp pointed knife cut a small thin cross on top of each tomato. Put them in heavily boiling water for a ½ minute and remove, then put them instantly in icecold water. That will cause the skin to loosen and make it is easy to peel it off. Cut them in two and remove all the seeds from inside.

Cut the tomatoes in even slices.

Peel the orange with a sharp peeling knife. It is important to remove all the peel until it is only the orange flesh. Cut out the segments of the oranges.

Squeeze all the juice out of the bulb.

Sauté the shallot and the garlic in a wide deep frying pan.

Add in the fennel and the orange juice. Let it all sauté together and add the stock. Let it boil slowly together for a few minutes to reduce.

Take off the heat and add the butter bit by bit, stirring constantly with a wooden spoon.

In the end, add the orange segments, the slice tomato slices and the shreddded tarragon leaves. Add salt and white pepper from the mill to taste. Keep hot without boiling.

Panfry the Arctic Char fillet in a non-stick pan in very little olive oil or butter. Salt and pepper to taste.

Arrange the fennel, orange and tomato broth in a deep plate and put the pan-fried fillets of Arctic Char on top of that.
Garnish with a sprig of tarragon.

BRAISED LEG OF LAMB WITH WHITE WINE, SAGE, TOMATOES AND MUSHROOMS
(4-6 SERVINGS)

INGREDIENTS:
1 leg of lamb, bone in
1 tbsp olive oil
1 tbsp butter
6 ripe tomatoes
4 shallots, chopped
2-3 carrots, cut in small dices
½ lb medium size mushrooms, cut in two
2 glasses white wine
2/3–1 pint lamb or chicken stock
2–3 branches fresh sage
salt and pepper from the mill

4-6 cloves of garlic
½ cup parsley
zest of 1 lemon (all chopped together)

PREPARATION:
Cut a small cross in skin of the plum tomatoes and put them in boiling hot water for 30 seconds. Then transfer them instantly into very cold water. The skin loosens and peels off easily. Slice the peeled tomatoes and arrange them in a medium deep oven-proof dish.

Sear the leg of lamb on all sides in olive oil in a frying pan over medium heat. Don´t clean the pan. Put the seared leg of lamb on top of the tomatoes.

Fry in the same pan the carrots, shallots and celery sticks in some butter and olive oil until tender. Add the mushrooms. Deglaze the pan with the white wine and the stock.

Pour the vegetables and the wine and stock over the leg of lamb and tomatoes. Put the sage leaves in between the tomatoes and the lamb.

Bake in the oven at approx. 220° F for about 1½-2 hours. Pour the stock occasionally over the leg of lamb. For the last 20 minutes in the oven, sprinkle the chopped garlic, parsley and lemon zest over the leg of lamb.

SKYR SOUFFLÉ ICE CREAM
(ABOUT 10 SERVINGS)

INGREDIENTS:
1/4 l egg whites (yolks combined with the skyr)
1/4 l 36% cream
300 g sugar
1/2 tsp vanilla drops
1/2 tsp vinegar
500 g skyr (=greek yoghurt)

PREPARATION:
Whip the cream and set aside.

Egg whites and 200 g of sugar are whipped stiff, put a little vinegar or lemon juice when it's ready.

Take the yolks, vanilla drops, 100 g of sugar and put it in the skyr. Combine the skyr mixture with the egg whites and sugar, then put in the cream.

Freeze the mixture in small ramekins.

ITALY

Recipes provided by Mrs Laura Denise Bisogniero,
spouse of the Deputy Secretary General of
the North Atlantic Treaty Organization

Vitello Tonnato 'My Way'

***

Summer Lasagna

***

Semifreddo di Amaretti

VITELLO TONNATO 'MY WAY' (TUNA VEAL, 10 SERVINGS)

After having cooked it for many years (it is a "classic" in the Italian hot summers!), I made some changes in the recipe. It is now much quicker to prepare, and very good, too.

Instead of using boiled veal, I prefer totally lean, fat free pork (900-1000 g), roasted in the hot oven for about an hour (it depends on the quantity) with a little olive oil and salt (it is more tasty!).

When cold, I slice it very thin and then place the slices flat on the serving plate, one next to the other, until the plate is fully covered.

INGREDIENTS OF THE SAUCE:
tuna fish in olive oil cans (well drained)
very small, crispy pickles in vinegar (well drained)
lemon juice
mayonnaise
capers and/or olives for decoration

PREPARATION:
For ten people, grind about 8–10 pickles, add 4 cans of well drained tuna fish (each can about 180 g) and grind while mixing. Add the juice of 2 lemons, mix, and add about 12 tbsp of mayonnaise. Mix well until it becomes creamy, and then keep in a well closed container in the refrigerator.
Some time before dinner starts, spread the sauce over the sliced meat and decorate with capers or olives.

Keep in the refrigerator until the moment you serve it.

SUMMER LASAGNA (8-10 SERVINGS)

INGREDIENTS:
about 250 g of dry Lasagna
900 g ricotta cheese
2.5 kg of fresh tomatoes
rocket salad (about 150 g)
1 tbsp olive oil
a little milk
salt
grated parmesan cheese

PREPARATION:
Skin the fresh tomatoes (it is easier if you plunge them for a few minutes in very hot water, a little quantity at a time) and cut them in slices. Drain the tomato flesh from the watery juice and seeds and keep them in separate containers.

Make the ricotta softer by mixing it with a little milk until it has the consistency of a thick cream and is easy to spread.

Boil the lasagna, a few at a time, in plenty of hot, salty water to which you will have added a table spoon of olive oil (this is important: the oil helps the lasagna not to stick together) as you would do with any kind of pasta and check the cooking time.

When ready, take them out of the water using a large flat spoon with holes and put them flat on a large moist canvas, each one separate from the other.

Only just before putting them in the pan (so that the fresh tomatoes do not get too watery!), mix sliced fresh tomatoes with olive oil and salt, and in a separate bowl do the same with the rocket salad.

Take a Lasagna-pan (shallow sides), lightly oiled, and pour a first layer of tomatoes, add a layer of Lasagna, spread some ricotta over this and add some rocket salad.

Make several layers like this and end with pieces of tomatoes and some spoonfuls of the tomato juice you kept aside.

Put in hot oven until pleasantly warm, but not too hot: it is a summer lasagna!

Serve with grated parmesan cheese if you like .

SEMIFREDDO DI AMARETTI (AMARETTO ICE CREAM)

Amarettini are Italian biscuits, invented in the early 1700s, when a Milan bishop surprised the town of Saronno with a visit. A young couple, residents of the town, welcomed him and paid tribute with an original confection: on the spur of the moment, they had baked biscuits made of sugar, egg whites, and crushed apricot kernels or almonds. These so pleased the visiting bishop that he blessed the two with a happy and lifelong marriage, resulting in the preservation of the secret recipe over many generations. Amarettini are still widely used for baking or eaten as delicious biscuits today. There is also a famous brand of liquor of that name, based on the biscuit.

INGREDIENTS:
200 g of Amaretti biscuits, ground (plus some more for decoration)
6 eggs yolks, whipped with 6 tablespoons of sugar
half a litre of thick cream, whipped, with 3 tablespoons of sugar (plus some more for decoration)

PREPARATION:
When the yolks and sugar are well whipped, fold the Amaretti delicately into the whipped cream.

Pour into a mould and put in the deep freezer. Better prepare it a day in advance.

Take it out some time before serving as you would do with any ice cream.

Decorate with more whipped cream and some Amaretti biscuits.

ITALY 2

Recipes contributed by Mrs Stephanie Stefanini,
spouse of the Italian Permanent Representative on
the North Atlantic Council

Trenette al Pesto

***

Orata al Forno

***

Panna Cotta con Mirtilli

I have decided to offer a menu typical of Liguria ..., the region my husband is from. Liguria includes the area known as the Italian Riviera and life largely revolves around the sea. Fishing for both business and pleasure plays an important role in the area and provides the basis for most typically Ligurian seaside menus. Liguria is also famous for pesto sauce and some restaurants even serve nothing but food prepared with pesto.

In an attempt to include both elements, I will start with a typical pesto pasta, followed by a main course of fish and a light summery dessert.

This of course will be finished off with home made limoncello, straight from the freezer.

TRENETTE AL PESTO (8 SERVINGS)

First, you must make your own pesto – it's easy!
This will be enough for 800 grams of pasta….. considering Italians estimate 100 grams per person.

INGREDIENTS:
50 fresh basil leaves
2 cloves of garlic
pinch of salt
2 tbsp of grated parmesan cheese
1 to 1 1/2 cups of extra virgin olive oil

100 g of green beans
1 potato
800 g of pasta

PREPARATION:
Put about 50 fresh basil leaves in a mortar together with 2 cloves of garlic and a pinch of salt.
Mix with the pestle – without pounding too much.

Little by little, add 2 tablespoons of grated parmesan cheese.
When a thick paste forms, transfer the mixture to a bowl and add 1 to 1 ½ cups of extra virgin olive oil according to taste.

Of course, you can always take the modern route and blend the basil, garlic, salt and parmesan in a blender and then add the oil afterwards. It will be more creamy – and less authentic!

Trenette are the Genovese version of fine pasta but in shorter pieces.

Boil enough salted water to cover the pasta.

In this water, first cook about 100 grams of green beans cut into pieces about 2 cm long, AND 1 decent sized potato, cut into tiny pieces of about the same size as the beans.

Let the vegetables cook and when they are almost ready, pour in the uncooked trenette and continue to boil until ready.

Strain the vegetables and trenette together and carefully stir in the pesto sauce.

When adding the sauce, it is always a good idea to drain the pasta and put it back into the pot in which it was cooked. This keeps it hot while you add the sauce. Then transfer to a serving bowl and sprinkle some extra parmesan on top – along with a few whole basil leaves.

ORAT AL FORNO WITH INSALATA MISTA (SEA BASS IN THE OVEN, 2 SERVINGS)

Ligurians pride themselves on fresh fish, "appena pescato" – just caught!!
I am a firm believer that fresh fish is best cooked very simply – let the flavour speak for itself.
Roasting fish is easy and helps keep it tender and moist. Usually, the fish is cooked whole in the oven with the head on. Orata are not big fish and can be served as 1 per person. Let's prepare 2.

INGREDIENTS:
2 cleaned, gutted Orata, heads intact.
2 tbsp olive oil
salt
freshly ground black pepper
1 lemon, cut into 8 wedges
1 coarsely chopped small onion
1 small chopped fennel
6 sprigs fresh rosemary
2 thinly sliced garlic cloves
sliced potatoes – as many as needed

PREPARATION:
Preheat the oven to 200 °C.

Line a heavy baking sheet with foil and coat with 1 tablespoon of the oil.

Place the whole fish on top and sprinkle the cavities with salt and pepper.

Squeeze lemon juice from 4 of the wedges inside and leave the wedges there.

Fill the cavities with onion, fennel, rosemary and garlic. Rub the remaining oil over the outside of the fish and sprinkle with more salt and pepper.
Place the potatoes around the fish and also sprinkle with salt and pepper and pieces of rosemary.

Roast in the oven until the fish is just cooked to the bone, about 40 minutes.

Pull the skin back from atop the fish and using a sharp knife, separate the two fillets from the backbone of each fish. They should come free easily, taking the heads with them, discard!

Using a spatula, transfer the fish and potatoes to a serving dish and decorate with extra slices of lemon.

A light salad is often used to accompany this dish.

PREPARATION:
Mix green salad of choice with tomatoes and sliced fennel and a few olives in a bowl. Add salt, a teaspoon or so of olive oil and a dash of lemon juice. Mix well.

PANNA COTTA CON MIRTILLI (COOKED CREAM AND FRESH BERRIES) WITH LIMONCELLO

INGREDIENTS:
1 cup whole milk
1 tbsp unflavoured powdered gelatine,
3 cups whipping cream
1/3 cup honey
1 tbsp sugar
pinch of salt
2 cups of berries of choice

PREPARATION:
Put the milk in a small, heavy saucepan.

Sprinkle the gelatine in the milk and let stand for 5 minutes to soften.
Stir over medium heat until the gelatine dissolves, but do not let the milk boil, about 5 minutes.

Add cream, sugar, honey and salt and stir until the sugar dissolves, about 2 minutes.

Remove from heat and let cool slightly.

Poor the mixture into glasses, cover and refrigerate until set.
Before serving, add berries on top of the panna cotta.

An added touch: place a biscotto on the side.

LIMONCELLO

LIMONCELLO – to be made WAY ahead of time!!

INGREDIENTS:
2 x 750 ml bottles of pure grain alcohol
zest of 15 lemons
3 cups white sugar
5 cups water

PREPARATION:
Take the zest off the lemons and add them to a glass jar with the alcohol. Leave for 6 weeks.

Mix sugar and water together in a pot and bring to a boil for 5 minutes. When completely cooled, mix with the lemon and alcohol. Let the mixture stand for another 6 weeks.

Filter a few times through a cloth or a normal paper coffee filter, bottle
and put in the freezer.

Enjoy!

LATVIA

Recipes provided by Mrs Brigita Eichmane,
spouse of the Latvian Permanent Representative on the
North Atlantic Council

Trout Cakes with Chive and Lemon Sauce

***

Roast Pork with Rye Bread and Bacon Cubes

***

Gooseberry Mousse with Whipping Cream

Cooking for me is not only necessity, but it is also a precious and gentle ritual which helps gather and hold families and friends together. Over centuries recipes were passed from generation to generation and ancient foods are still eaten by Latvians daily and on special occasions.

The most typical ancient foods eaten by Latvians are still found today at traditional Latvian celebrations. These celebrations are related to annual seasonal events, and to the rhythm of farming in the northern hemisphere, which is dependent on the solar year. This is why Latvian food and drink at traditional celebrations are those which are the most convenient to prepare at any given time of the year.

Today the most popular celebration in Latvia is JANI or the summer solstice. This marks the shortest night of the year, when throughout Latvia special JANI folk songs are sung, floral wreaths are made, and countless bonfires burn until the morning. The main JANI foods are fresh caraway cheese and beer, which is found on every JANI festive table. Usually the table will also be laden with PIRAGI, sweet platter breads, various meats and many other modern foods, which suit contemporary Latvian celebrations. What is most important is passionate respect for using fresh local products and enjoying the results with friends.

I would like to offer a three-course meals from my family recipe book and some of my favourite, very traditional Latvian recipes.

TROUT CAKES WITH CHIVE AND LEMON SAUCE

INGREDIENTS:
300 g trout, skin and bones removed
1/4 teaspoon salt
pinch of black pepper
1 egg
2/3 cup whipping cream
3/4 cup milk
fresh flat-leaf parsley leaves, to garnish

PREPARATION:
Preheat the oven to 160 °C. Prepare four individual soufflé dishes. Grease the moulds, then line them with rounds of waxed paper and brush the lining with softened butter, pressing out any air holes. Press one or two parsley leaves, then refrigerate.

To make the cake mixture, cut the trout into small cubes and place in a food processor with the salt, black pepper and egg. Blend until smooth. Add the cream and milk. Push the mixture through a strainer into a pitcher.

Pour the mixture into the moulds, tapping them on a work surface to remove any bubbles. Fill the pan with boiling water so that it rises halfway up the sides of the moulds; transfer to the oven and bake for 15-20 minutes.

Remove from the hot water bath and allow to rest. Keep warm.

INGREDIENTS for chive and lemon sauce:
1 shallot, finely chopped
juice of 1 lemon
2/3 cup unsalted butter, chilled and cut into small cubes
1 tbsp very finely chopped fresh chives

PREPARATION:
To make a chive and lemon sauce, place the shallot and lemon juice in a small saucepan. Add 2 tablespoons water, bring to a boil and reduce for about 5 minutes. Reduce the heat to low, then whisk in the butter, a few pieces at a time, without letting the sauce boil. Strain into a clean saucepan and season to taste with salt and pepper. Before serving, whisk in the chives.

Loosen the cakes from the inside of the moulds using a knife. Gently unmould the cakes onto individual serving plates. Drizzle the sauce around and serve immediately.

ROAST PORK WITH RYE BREAD AND BACON CUBES

INGREDIENTS:
1 cup rye bread cubes
1 cup smoked bacon cubes
1.3 kg loin of pork bones removed
3 tbsp unsalted butter

PREPARATION:
Preheat the oven to 180 °C. Remove the skin and excess sinew from the pork, leaving a thin layer of fat. Cut a long slit down to halfway through the meat. Gently push the mixture of rye bread and bacon cubes into the slit. Close and roll the flat flap around the loin. Tie pieces of string 3 cm apart along the loin to hold it together.

Heat the butter in a frying pan. Add the pork and fry over medium-high heat for 6-7 minutes, until sealed and browned all over. Transfer to a roasting pan and roast for 1-1 1/2 hours, until the juices run clear when pierced with a skewer.

INGREDIENTS for herb sauce:
2 large shallots, chopped
2 cups chicken stock
1 cup whipping cream
1 1/2 tbsp fresh dill, finely chopped

PREPARATION:
To make the herb sauce, melt the butter in a saucepan, add shallots and cook, covered, over low heat for 5 minutes, until soft and translucent. Pour the stock and simmer for 15-20 minutes, then stir in the cream and simmer until the sauce lightly coats the back of a spoon. Remove from heat, cover the surface and keep warm.

Transfer the pork from the oven to a plate and let rest for 5 minutes, then place on a cutting board. Gently reheat the sauce, but do not allow it to bubble for more than 1 minute. Add the dill and parsley and season with salt and black pepper just before serving. Remove the string from the meat and cut the pork into slices. Arrange the slices on plates and pour the sauce around. Serve with potatoes and green salad or seasonal vegetables.

GOOSEBERRY MOUSSE WITH WHIPPING CREAM

Dessert made of cooked, strained and pureed fruit, chilled and folded into custard and whipped cream.

INGREDIENTS:
4 cups fresh gooseberries, trimmed at both ends
1/2 tsp gelatine
3/4 cup sugar
2 tbsp potato starch or cornstarch
1/4 cup sugar
1/2 cup milk
3/4 cup whipping cream
1 egg white
1/4 cup whipping cream, to serve

PREPARATION:
To make the purée, reserve 1 tablespoon of sugar and place the rest in a heavy-bottomed saucepan with 1 cup water. Stir over low heat until sugar dissolves. Bring to a boil, add the fruit, reduce the heat and simmer for 10 minutes, or until tender.

Strain off the liquid. Purée the fruit in a food processor, then stir in the reserved sugar.

Soak the gelatine. Allow to soak for a few minutes.

In a separate heatproof bowl, combine the potato starch and 1 tablespoon of the sugar. Add 1/4 cup of the milk and stir until smooth. Bring the remaining milk almost to a boil, then quickly remove from the heat and whisk it into potato starch and sugar. Place in a clean pan and whisk over low heat until mixture boils and thickens. Remove from heat.

Stir the soaked gelatine into the hot custard until dissolved, then cover with parchment paper and allow to cool. Stir in the fruit purée.

Whip the cream until soft peaks form, then fold into the custard. Whisk the egg white in a clean, dry bowl until stiff, then whisk in the remaining sugar and fold into the custard.

Spoon the mousse into dessert glasses, ensuring there are no air pockets. Chill for 2 hours to set.

Serve with some freshly whipped cream.

LITHUANIA

Recipes provided by Mrs Danguole Linkeviciene, spouse of the Lithuanian Permanent Representative on the North Atlantic Council

Chicken Jelly with Red Salad

***

Cabbage Wraps with Meat or Vegetable Filling

***

Baked Apples

CHICKEN JELLY WITH RED SALAD

INGREDIENTS:
1 medium chicken
1.5 litres water
2 onions
6 peppercorns
2 bay leaves
2 tsp salt
5 tsp gelatine

PREPARATION:
Take the chicken, cut it up into small pieces and put it in the pot filled with 1.5 litres of water, seasoned with 2 teaspoons salt. Bring to a boil, skim the scum with a skimming ladle, add the peppers, the onions, bay leaves and keep it boiling for 60 minutes on medium heat. Remove the meat and strain the liquid through a fine sieve into a bowl. Take the meat off the bones and cut it up into very small pieces.

Put the gelatine in a jar, fill it with one cup of cold water and keep for 15 minutes till it swells up. Set the jar in the kettle with hot water and bring the gelatine to the boil, stirring constantly. Then pour it into the bowl of liquid.

Put the meat into plastic cups (it is very easy to take out later), pour on the liquid and put in the fridge to gel. You can add some green peas or parsley springs on the bottom of the cups to make it look nicer.
After 30 minutes the chicken jelly is ready. You just need to take it out of the cups.

RED SALAD

INGREDIENTS:
3 carrots
100 g white beans
3 beets
2 pickled cucumbers
4 tbsp cooking oil
1 onion
pepper
salt

PREPARATION:
Boil the carrots, beans and beets separately. Peel the carrots and beets and cut them up into very small pieces. Cut up the cucumbers, too. Put all the vegetables into a big bowl, add some pepper and salt and mix it all up. Chop up the onion, put in the saucepan with oil and fry until it is a golden colour.

Then pour the mixture on top of the vegetables and mix it all up.

CABBAGE WRAPS WITH MEAT OR VEGETABLE FILLING

INGREDIENTS:
1 medium cabbage
1 carrot
2 tbsp tomato paste
0.5 cup flour
0.5 cup sour cream
bay leaf, meat stock
1 tbsp cooking oil

PREPARATION:
Put the cabbage into a big pot, pour some water in and add salt. Let it boil until the leaves become a bit tender and it is easy to take them off. Do not overcook!!!

Take some meat or vegetable filling and wrap it into a cabbage leaf. Repeat. Sprinkle some flour over the wraps and fry in the pan until they get light brown.

Then put the wraps in the pot, add some chopped carrots, bay leaf and meat stock. When it boils for 10 minutes, add tomato paste and let it simmer for about 30 minutes. Add some salt and pepper if you like.

Serve with boiled potatoes and sour cream.

INGREDIENTS for meat Filling:
500 g ground beef
0.5 cup rice
1 finely chopped onion
0.5 tsp pepper
1 tsp salt

PREPARATION:
Mix all ingredients together and the filling is ready. You can use boiled rice, too.

INGREDIENTS for vegetable filling:
5 carrots
3 onions
0.5 cup rice
1 egg
1 tbsp butter
1 tsp salt
1 tsp pepper
dill and parsley

PREPARATION:
Peel the carrots and grate them, chop onions and fry all these ingredients in the saucepan with some butter for a few minutes. Add some pepper and salt, too. Let it cool.
Then put in half of the cooked rice, an egg, some dill, parsley and mix it
well.

BAKED APPLES

INGREDIENTS:
5 apples
40 g almond flakes
2 cinnamon sticks
3 tbsp honey
3 cloves
2 tbsp butter

PREPARATION:
Remove the core from each apple without cutting all the way through. Place the apples in a baking dish. Fill the holes with the honey and almond mix and smear the apples with some butter.
Put in the oven and bake for 40 minutes at 180 °C until the apples are tender.

Serve hot or warm, topping each apple with a teaspoon (or more) of ice cream.

Enjoy!

LUXEMBOURG

Recipe found at: www.alleasyrecipes.com

Quetsche Tort

***

QUETSCHE TORT (PLUM TART WITH CURRANT JELLY)

INGREDIENTS:
Pastry:
1 1/3 cups plus 2 tbsp flour
1 tbsp sugar
3 egg yolks
8 tbsp (1 quarter-pound stick) plus 1 tbsp unsalted butter, softened
2 tsp finely grated fresh lemon peel

Filling:
3 pounds firm ripe plums, cut lengthwise in half and pitted
½ cup red or black currant jelly

PREPARATION:
Combine 1 1/3 cups of the flour and the sugar, and sift them into a deep bowl. Make a well in the center, drop in the egg yolks and, stirring gently, gradually incorporate the flour into the yolks.

Beat in 8 tablespoons of the softened butter, 1 tablespoon at a time, then add the lemon peel and continue to beat until the dough is smooth and pliable. Gather the dough into a ball, wrap in wax paper, and refrigerate for at least 30 minutes.

With a pastry brush, spread the 1 tablespoon of softened butter evenly over the bottom and sides of a 9-inch false-bottomed fluted quiche pan.

Sprinkle 2 tablespoons of flour over the butter and tip the pan from side to side to spread the flour evenly. Invert the pan and rap the bottom sharply to remove the excess flour.

On a lightly floured surface, pat the dough into a circle about 1 inch thick. Dust a little flour over and under it and roll it out into a circle about 13 to 14 inches in diameter and 1/8 inch thick. Drape the dough over the rolling pin, lift it up and unroll it slackly over the prepared pan.
Gently press the dough into the bottom and against the sides of the pan. Roll the pin over the rim of the pan, pressing down hard to trim off the excess pastry. Chill the pastry-lined pan for 30 minutes or more.

Preheat the oven to 375 °F. Arrange the plum halves, cut side up, in concentric circles in the pastry-lined pan. If the plums are small, it may be necessary to arrange them in two layers. Bake in the middle of the oven for 1 hour, or until the tart is brown and the plums are tender.
Remove the tart from the oven, set the pan on a large jar or can and slip down the outside rim. Let cool to room temperature, then run a large metal spatula under the tart to loosen the bottom, and slide the tart off onto a serving plate.

Before serving, heat the jelly in a small pan until it melts. With the back of a spoon, rub the jelly through a fine sieve into a small bowl. Then, with a pastry brush, glaze the surface of the plums with the jelly while it is still warm. Set the tart aside to cool to room temperature but do not refrigerate.

THE NETHERLANDS

Recipes provided by Mrs Vivian Voss Schaper, spouse of the Permanent Representative of the Netherlands on the North Atlantic Council

Koninginnesoep

***

Gehaktballen

***

Appeltjes onder de deken

KONINGINNESOEP (QUEEN'S SOUP)

INGREDIENTS:
1 litre (2 pints) chicken stock
30 g (1 oz) flour
150 g (5 oz) smoked salmon, in pieces
freshly ground pepper
a pinch of nutmeg
a few drops of lemon juice
1 egg yolk
100 ml (3 ½ fl oz) cream
2 tbsp freshly chopped dill

PREPARATION:
Heat the chicken stock. Melt the butter in a large saucepan and stir in the flour. Pour the stock into the cooked flour, stirring all the while, and simmer gently for about 10 minutes.

Season the soup with pepper, nutmeg and lemon juice.

Beat the egg yolk with the cream and stir in 5 tablespoons of the hot soup. Remove the pan from the heat and stir the mixture into the soup.

Sprinkle with salmon and dill before serving.

VARIATION:
Substitute 300 g (10 oz) chicken cubes for the salmon and heat through in the soup. Garnish with fresh chives instead of dill.

GEHAKTBALLEN (MEATBALLS)

INGREDIENTS:
1 onion
2 cloves garlic
75 g (3 oz) butter
100 g (3 ½ oz) smoked bacon, diced
2 tsp finely chopped rosemary
2 slices stale white bread
100 ml (3 1/2fl oz) milk
1 egg
500 g (1 lb) beef and pork mince
salt and pepper, breadcrumbs

PREPARATION:
Peel and finely chop the onion and garlic.

Heat half the butter in a frying pan and fry the diced bacon. Add the onion and garlic and sauté until translucent. Add the rosemary and fry for about 3 more minutes.

Trim the crusts from the bread and soak in milk. Squeeze the bread out and mix it with the bacon mixture and the egg and the mince. Season the mince to taste and shape into 8 balls and roll these in the breadcrumbs.

Heat the rest of the butter in a large casserole and sauté the meatballs until brown on all sides. Reduce heat and cook for about 20 minutes, partly covered with a lid, until done. Turn occasionally.

APPELTJES ONDER DE DEKEN (APPLES UNDER THE BLANKETS)

INGREDIENTS:
4 Cox's Orange apples
50 g (2 oz) raisins
80 g (3 oz) sugar
1 tsp cinnamon
25 g (1 oz) butter
40 g ((1 ½ oz) custard powder
800 ml (1 ½) milk

PREPARATION:
Preheat the oven to 175 °C (375 °F).
Peel and core the fruit with an apple corer. In a bowl, mix the raisins with the cinnamon and 2 tablespoons of sugar. Stuff the mixture into the centres of the apples.
Lay the apples side by side in a greased shallow oven dish. Dot each apple with butter and bake for about 30 minutes until done.

In a small bowl, blend the custard powder and remaining sugar with 100 ml (2 ½ fl oz) milk into a smooth paste. Bring the rest of the milk to the boil in a pan and add the custard paste, stirring all the while. Continue stirring until the custard is thick and smooth.

Spoon the custard sauce over the apples and serve hot.

VARIATION:
Add freshly chopped balls of stem ginger, Amaretti biscuits or pecan nuts to the raisin stuffing. Place the apples in separate oven dishes. When baked, pour fresh chilled custard sauce over the apples.

NORWAY

Recipes contributed by Mrs Astrid Brodtkorb, spouse of the Norwegian Permanent Representative on the North Atlantic Council

Norwegian Gravlaks
with Mustard Sauce
and Stewed Potatoes

***

NORWEGIAN GRAVLAKS - CURED SALMON

Gravlaks is a simple way of preparing salmon that produces an excellent dish with clean flavours and remarkable texture. In Norway it is served as an appetizer on toast with mustard dill sauce, or as a main dish together with the sauce and stewed potatoes.

Gravlaks literally means "buried salmon", referring to the old, traditional method of preparation, where the fresh salmon was heavily salted and buried in dry sand to ferment and cure.

Today, for safety, we always prepare the gravlaks from salmon that has been frozen. The freezing kills parasites that might naturally reside in fresh salmon.

If you are going to fillet the salmon yourself, it is easiest to do it before it is completely thawed. The fillets should be cut parallel to the backbone. Remove bones with pliers.
It does not need to be scaled.

INGREDIENTS:
1 salmon (4 – 6 pounds)
3 tbsp vegetable oil
2 tbsp spirits – whisky, cognac, aquavit etc. (optional)
4 tbsp sugar
5 tbsp salt
1 tbsp crushed, white pepper
3 bunches dill

PREPARATION:
Combine the spirit and oil, and rub it into the fillets.

Combine the salt, sugar and pepper. Spoon it onto both sides of the fillets.

Cover a big plate with one bunch of dill. Put one salmon fillet skin-side down on the dill. Cover the fillet with a bunch of dill. Put the other fillet on top, skin-side up. Cover with one bunch of dill.

Put light pressure on top of the fillets and refrigerate for 2–3 days. Turn the fillets once or twice a day.

Scrape the fillets clean of dill and spices and slice thinly.
Sprinkle with freshly cut dill. Serve with mustard sauce on toast as a starter, or with mustard sauce and and stewed potatoes as a main course.

MUSTARD SAUCE

INGREDIENTS:
4 tbsp plain mustard
1 tbsp Dijon mustard
1 egg yolk
2 tbsp sugar
2 tbsp white wine vinegar
2/3 cup extra virgin olive oil
4–5 tbsp freshly chopped dill

PREPARATION:
Mix all the ingredients, apart from the dill and the oil.

Mix in the oil – start one drop at a time, go slowly so the sauce doesn't separate. Mix in the freshly chopped dill.

Refrigerate.

STEWED POTATOES

INGREDIENTS:
12 medium potatoes
3–4 sprigs of dill
1 tbsp butter
½ tbsp nutmeg
2 tbsp plain flour
1 ¼ milk
Salt and pepper to taste
2 tbsp freshly chopped dill

PREPARATION:
Peel the potatoes and chop them into half inch cubes. Boil them in water with the dill sprigs and salt until they are cooked through.

Make the béchamel sauce: Melt butter in a saucepan over medium-high heat until it foams. Sprinkle in the nutmeg and add flour. Cook, stirring, for 1 to 2 minutes, remove from heat. Slowly add milk, whisking constantly until mixture is smooth. Return to heat. Cook over low heat, stirring with a wooden spoon, for approx. 10 minutes, or until the sauce comes to a boil, thickens and coats the back of the wooden spoon. Remove from heat, sprinkle with salt and pepper to taste. Add the boiled potatoes and freshly chopped dill.

Vel bekomme! - as we say in Norway

POLAND

Recipes provided by Mrs Beata Winid,
spouse of the Polish Permanent Representative on the
North Atlantic Council

Fresh Salmon Tartar on Potato Pancakes

***

Cold Cucumber Soup with Fresh Mint

***

Rolled Wild-Boar Fillet with Forest Mushroom Sauce

***

Potato Dumplings with Plum and Orange Jam

FRESH SALMON TARTAR ON POTATO PANCAKES

INGREDIENTS:
0.4 kg fresh salmon fillet
2 tbsp capers
2 red onions
2 tbsp fresh dill, chopped
1 tbsp fresh basil, chopped
4-6 tbsp olive oil
1 lemon (juice)
salt, pepper

PREPARATION:
Cut the salmon into very small cubes. Mix with capers, red onion (cut into small cubes), add dill, basil, lemon juice, salt and pepper.

Serve on potato pancakes.

INGREDIENTS for potato pancakes:
1 kg potatoes
1 fresh onion
1 egg
4 tbsp flour
salt
olive oil

PREPARATION:
Grate potato and onion. Mix eggs, grated potatoes and onions, flour, salt and pepper.
Fry in heated oil on each side until crisp.

COLD CUCUMBER SOUP WITH FRESH MINT

INGREDIENTS:
0.5 l yoghurt
0.5 l buttermilk
0.5 l kefir
3 fresh cucumbers
3 tbsp fresh dill, chopped
3 tbsp fresh chives, chopped
4 leaves fresh mint, chopped
2 cloves fresh garlic
3-4 tbsp olive oil
1 lemon (juice)
salt, sugar, pepper
quail egg

PREPARATION:
Peel, seed and grate the cucumbers. Mix with yoghurt, kefir and buttermilk.

Add dill, chives, mint and mashed garlic. Finally, add salt, pepper, fresh lemon juice and olive oil.

Serve cold with boiled quail egg.

ROLLED WILD-BOAR FILLET WITH FOREST MUSHROOM SAUCE

INGREDIENTS:
0.5 kg wild-boar haunch
1 fresh carrot
0.15 kg bacon

MARINADE:
1 fresh carrot
1 bunch of fresh parsley
1 fresh celery
1 onion
0.3 l red wine
0.1 l cherry vodka
0.05 l olive oil
salt, sugar, juniper, pepper seeds

SAUCE:
0.25 kg fresh chanterelle mushrooms
0.5 l whole cream
2 onions, chopped
2 cloves of fresh garlic
2-3 tbsp butter
1 lemon (zest)

PREPARATION:
Wash and dry the meat.

Prepare the marinade:
Cut carrot, parsley and celery into slices, add crushed pepper seeds, salt, sugar, juniper and combine with the mixed-up red wine, cherry vodka and olive oil.

Put the meat in the marinade for 24 hours, turning over 2–3 times

Cut the boar haunch into slices. Beat the meat, add salt and pepper. Put the carrot slices on each piece of meat and roll them. Wrap the meat with the bacon. Dip the rolled meat in the flour. Put some olive oil in a baking pan. Place the floured meat in the pan. Quick-fry, then add some bouillon and stew under the cover.

Cook chanterelle mushrooms in small amount of salted water. Fry onion with the butter, after 2 minutes add cooked and chopped chanterelle mushrooms, mashed garlic, whole sour cream, salt and pepper. After 1-2 minutes add lemon zest. Sauce is ready.

Serve with buckwheat.

POTATO DUMPLINGS WITH PLUM AND ORANGE JAM

INGREDIENTS:
1.5 kg potatoes
1.3 kg farmer cheese
0.5 kg flour
0.3 kg potato flour
0.3 kg sugar
2 eggs
2 tbsp vanilla sugar
salt
1 jar orange jam
1.5 kg fresh plums
2 tbsp cinnamon
0.1 kg bread crumbs
vanilla sauce

PREPARATION:
Cook whole potatoes. When they are done, let them cool and mash them. Mix the potatoes with farmers cheese, flour, potato flour, sugar (0.2 kg), vanilla sugar, salt.

Remove pits from the plums.

Boil water. Take a little dough and place it around plum and orange jam to make a little ball. Put them in the boiling water – they are done when they start floating. Take them out and roll them into mixed bread crumbs, cinnamon and sugar (0.1 kg).

Serve with vanilla sauce.

PORTUGAL

Recipes provided by Mrs Maria José Morais Pires,
spouse of the Portugese Permanent Representative on
the North Atlantic Council

Prawn Soup

***

Cod Fish

***

Orange Roll

PRAWN SOUP (6-8 SERVINGS)

INGREDIENTS:
500 g prawns
1 carrot, sliced
1 large onion, chopped
1 clove garlic, chopped
10 ml butter
1 bay leaf
10 ml olive oil
60 ml white wine
2 tomatoes, peeled and grated
100 ml toasted flour
1 stick celery, sliced
10 ml port wine
5 ml chopped parsley
salt and pepper

PREPARATION:
Cook the prawns in boiling salted water for 3-4 minutes. Drain, and keep the water. Shell the prawns, reserving the heads and the shells.

Fry the chopped onion in the butter and olive oil until soft. Add the tomatoes, prawn heads and shells, celery, parsley, carrot, garlic, bay leaf and wine. Simmer for 10 minutes. Add the drained water and simmer for a further 30 minutes. Blend in batches in a blender and strain to remove any hard bits of shell.

Make a paste by mixing the toasted flour with a little water. Add to

the soup. Bring to the boil.
Chop 250 g of the prawns and add to the soup with the port wine.

Season to taste and serve with croutons.

To toast the flour, place the flour on a baking tray and bake at 180 °C until brown, stirring twice.

COD FISH (BACALHAU ESPIRITUAL, 5 SERVINGS)

INGREDIENTS:
400 g dry cod fish (bacalhau)
300 g carrots
300 g onions
4 cloves garlic
2 bread rolls
250 ml hot milk
15 ml manteiga (=butter)
125 grated cheese (optional)
125 bread crumbs

PREPARATION:
Soak the bacalhau overnight.

Drain and remove bones and skin.

Mince or chop the fish very finely, or chop in a food processor.

Chop the carrots, onions and garlic (this can also be done in a food processor).

Soak the bread in the hot milk.

Using a deep frying pan, heat the oil and butter and sauté the vegetables until soft and golden; add the fish;

Stir until all ingredients are well mixed;

Add the soaked bread and mix well.

INGREDIENTS for white sauce:
100 g butter
90 g flour
1 litre milk
4 eggs, separated
salt and pepper

PREPARATION:
Melt the butter and add the flour. Cook for a few minutes.

Add the milk. Mix well and bring to the boil, stirring continuously.

Add the beaten egg yolks, season.

Divide the sauce in half.

Add the first half to the fish mixture. Pour into greased oven-proof dish.

Whisk the egg whites until stiff, add to the remaining white sauce and pour over the mixture in the dish. Sprinkle with the grated cheese and bread crumbs, dot with butter.

Bake in a hot oven (190 °C) for about 15 minutes or until brown.

ORANGE ROLL (8-10 SERVINGS)

INGREDIENTS:
8 large eggs, separated
200 g sugar
150 g flour
sugar
10 ml grated orange rind

Syrup:
100 g sugar
50 ml water
100 ml orange juice
25 ml orange marmelade
1 tot orange liquor

PREPARATION:
Whisk the egg yolks with the sugar until pale. Fold in the stiffly beaten egg whites, and then fold in the flour. Pour into a lined Swiss-roll pan and bake at 190 °C for 10-15 minutes.

Meanwhile, make the syrup. Boil the sugar and water for 5 minutes. Remove from the heat and add the orange juice, marmalade and liquor.

Turn the cooked roll on to a cloth sprinkled with sugar. Pour half the syrup evenly over the roll. Roll up quickly and leave to cool. Transfer the roll to a serving dish and pour over the remaining syrup. Decorate with grated orange rind.

ROMANIA

Recipes provided by Mrs Carmen Ducaru,
spouse of the Romanian Permanent Representative on
the North Atlantic Council

Pickled Carp with Polenta

***

Lamb Roulade with Purée of Parsnip and three Sauces of Peppers

***

'Papanasi' with Cheese and Sour Cream

PICKLED CARP WITH POLENTA (REGIONAL DISH FROM THE DANUBE DELTA; 10 SERVINGS)

INGREDIENTS:
1.3 kg carp (fillet, no bones)
2 pieces hot chilli peppers
200 g tomatoes cut in small cubes
100 g green peppers cut in very fine slices
50 g garlic
1 bunch of dill
200 g coarse salt
1.5 l water
500 g corn flour

PREPARATION:
Roast the carp on a layer of coarse salt until it turns a golden-brown colour, then rinse with plenty of cold water. Separately, boil all the other ingredients in salty water, adding at the end the crushed garlic.

You serve it with polenta made by boiling corn meal with water, stirring continuously until it is soft and creamy.

LAMB ROULADE WITH PURÉE OF PARSNIP AND THREE SAUCES OF PEPPERS (TRADITIONAL ROMANIAN EASTER DISH, 10 SERVINGS)

INGREDIENTS:
1.2 kg joint of lamb
1 bunch of aromatic herbs (green basil, green onion, fresh garlic)
300 g parsnip
200 g celery root
150 g potatoes
300 g fresh liquid cream
1 yellow pepper
1 red pepper
1 green pepper
200 ml soup of lamb
100 ml white wine
salt, pepper

PREPARATION:
Cut the joint of the lamb, take out the bones sprinkle it with half of the aromatic herbs and spices and then roll it and tie it tightly with kitchen thread. Roast the meat with the rest of spices, flambé with 100 ml white wine, let the wine evaporate and then bake in the oven for approximately 35 minutes, adding the lamb soup.

Meanwhile, prepare the purée of parsnip: boil the roots with the fresh cream (100ml) and water; when they are done, blend all the vegetables. For the three sauces, you have to boil separately the peppers (by colour!) with the rest of the fresh cream, blend it in a mixer until the sauce has a semi-fluidic cosistency!

Serve the sauce on a plate, together with the roulade and the purée.

PAPANASI WITH CHEESE AND SOUR CREAM (10 SERVINGS)

INGREDIENTS:
700 g sweet cheese (ricotta)
500 g flour
5 g bicarbonate of soda
5 eggs
250 g sugar
sunflower oil
5 ml rum
500 g fresh sour cream
150 g fresh berries to decorate the dessert

PREPARATION:
Mix all the ingredients except the sour cream, 100 grams of sugar and the berries. Make the shape of a ring (papanași shape).

After 15 minutes, fry the rings in the hot sunflower oil until they are crisp.

Make the sauce, stirring the sour cream with the rest of the sugar.

You serve them hot, sprinkled with sugar, garnished with fresh berries and the sour cream sauce.

My favourite dessert!

by Cezar Munteanu
PRIVATE CHEF, CULINARY CONSULTING
www.chefcezar.com

SLOVAKIA

Recipes contributed by Mrs Alena Kasická,
spouse of the Slovak Permanent Representative on
the North Atlantic Council

Bryndza Dumplings (Bryndzove halusky)

***

Kettle Goulash (Kotlikovy Gulás)

***

Pirohy

BRYNDZA DUMPLINGS (BRYNDZOVE HALUSKY, 6 SERVINGS)

Probably every Slovak would mention this meal as the first choice when asked to name a Slovak national meal.

Bryndza is a special cheese made from sheep's milk. It can be replaced by cottage cheese made from cow's milk but then it cannot be called Bryndzove halusky in Slovakia any more – it is then Halusky s tvarohom (dumplings with cottage cheese).

INGREDIENTS:
1 kg of potatoes
200 g of flour
2 eggs
250 g of bryndza (a Slovak ewe cheese)
120 g of cubes of bacon
oil
milk
salt

PREPARATION:
Grate the raw potatoes, add some spoons of milk, the eggs and the flour in order to make a dough or mixture which is not too tough but not watery. Salt and mix. Knead the dough: it must be supple. Make rolls and cut small slices on a moistened plank.

Bring a big pan of salt water to a boil. Boil the slices in small numbers.

When they come back up, cook 5 or 6 minutes. Pick them out with a strainer, rinse with cold water and drain. Serve with crumbled bryndza.

Cut up little pieces of smoked bacon and fry them. Coat the dumplings with a lot of oil and add the fried cubes of bacon on top of the meal.

People usually serve Bryndzove halusky with a cup of ordinary milk.

KETTLE GOULASH (KOTLIKOVY GULÁS)

Gulás is traditionally made in late spring or during the summer holidays. Friends and family meet up in the woods and sit around an open fire where the Gulás is cooked. We sing songs, play games, drink and have fun, then eat a hearty meal.

This recipe brings up lots of lovely memories of being together with family and friends.

INGREDIENTS:
1 kg of beef and 0.5 kg of pork shoulder
2 kg of potatoes
1 kg of onions
2 fresh green peppers
3-4 tomatoes
2 dl of oil
1 dl of white or red wine (or 0.5 dl of brandy)
2 cloves of garlic
2 oxo cubes (1x vegetable, 1x meat)
2 tsp of salt
2 tbsp of sweet red paprika
1tsp of spicy red paprika
1 tbsp of cumin
1 tbsp of vegeta (dried herbs)
1 tsp of marjoram
½ tsp of ground black pepper
70 g of tomato purée

PREPARATION:
Begin by putting oil into a large pot, together with the diced onions and a sprinkle of salt. Also add fresh peppers, cut into thin strips, together with the diced tomatoes. Let this simmer for about 5-10 minutes. When the onions are ready, you should add the beef first, which you have cut into cubes beforehand. Then simmer for half an hour, stirring occasionally and pouring wine/brandy and hot water as you go. Then add cumin to taste.

After half an hour add the pork, which should also be cut into cubes, together with the garlic, the sweet and spicy paprika, the black pepper, the oxo cubes, the vegeta and the tomato purée.

When the meat is tender add the cubed potatoes and bring everything back to a boil. Add majoram and two grated potatoes to help thicken the gulás. Then let it cook until the potatoes are also tender, stirring it occasionally so that it doesn't burn.

Once the gulás is cooked, you can serve it with fresh bread.

PIROHY

INGREDIENTS:
2 cups flour
2 eggs
1 tsp salt
about 8 tbsp of cold water
warm water (enough for a large pot for boiling)
butter (to taste)

PREPARATION:
'Pirohy' is a traditional Eastern Slovak dish, which resembles large ravioli with a potato or cheese filling.

The first step of this recipe is to prepare the pastry from which we create the pirohy. Mix the flour, eggs and salt. Add enough warm water to make medium soft dough. Knead until blisters appear. Then roll the pastry out until it is half a centimeter thick. Divide into two portions. Roll out one portion thinly on a very lightly floured board sprinkled with a little salt. Cut in two-inch squares or create circle shapes (take a cup or glass and cut out circles from the pastry). This should make approximately 100 pirohy.

Place 1 teaspoon of the desired filling (see below) on each. Fold in half to make a triangle. Pinch edges well to keep filling from escaping. Follow the same method for the remaining portion of dough.

So now the pirohy are ready to be placed into a pot of boiling water. We put them into boiling water and stir them occasionally. We have to be very careful when we stirr them that we don't break them.

And when do we know that they have been cooked sufficiently? It is easy: when they float to the top we know they are ready to come back out again (takes about 10 minutes). Then cook about 5 minutes more. When done, pour a small amount of cold water over pirohy and drain. Put in a large serving bowl. Brown butter in skillet and pour over pirohy. Toss or mix well.

Cheese filling: 1 lb dry cottage cheese (mashed with fork), 1 egg yolk (beaten), 2 tbsp sugar, vanilla. Combine ingredients.

Potato filling: 1 large potato, cubed and cooked until tender. Drain. Mash cooked potato with mild cheddar cheese to taste and add 1 tsp of salt. Do not add milk to potatoes. They taste best when they are garnished with fried onions and served with sour cream.

SLOVENIA

Recipes provided by Mrs Martina Skok,
spouse of the Permanent Representative of Slovenia on
the North Atlantic Council

Vegetable Trio

***

Sea Bass 'Piran' with Chanterelles on a Buckwheat Bed

***

Lamb Fillet with Rosemary on Cream Purée with Glazed Shallot

***

Chestnut Tart

CUISINE IN SLOVENE DIPLOMATIC RESIDENCES

Slovenia is a small, but geographically rather variegated country. In the north, there are the Alps; in the south, it touches the Adriatic Sea; the central part consists of karst plateaus; and in the north-east it descends into the Pannonian Plain. Therefore, the food is varied and characterized by the neighbouring Mediterranean, Alpine and Central-European cuisines.

The oldest mentions of meal preparation and the hospitality of people in what today is Slovenia can be found in the writings of monks and travellers of the Middle Ages, and in various tales and fables. They reveal that Slovene food used to be tailored either to the seasons and the religious calendar – above all, in monasteries and more religious families – or to everyday living conditions. The less well-to-do classes prepared simple dishes, including various types of starchy food, bread, home-grown fruit, vegetables and meat from home-bred small cattle. The nobility and other households, which frequently received guests, used game, fish, various sorts of fruit and vegetables, meat and mostly Mediterranean spices.

Nowadays, the reception of guests in Slovene diplomatic residences differs from host to host. In all probability, we have similar place settings, serving dishes, cutlery, crystal, and lace tablecloths, while all the rest is left to the taste, imagination and inventiveness of each host. Most of us usually follow examples we know from tradition and the environments in which we grew up, but we often have to adapt to the current milieu, since there are sometimes no cooks abroad who are able to prepare Slovene food for larger groups of people.

On the other hand, various international sources today offer a number of recipes for traditional Slovene dishes, so anyone can try them. One of the best known is potica – a roulade of leavened dough, filled with nuts and raisins. Other renowned Slovene dishes are štruklji – cooked cottage cheese rolls, kranjska klobasa – Kransky sausage, the Soča River marble trout, and prekmurska gibanica – a layered cake from Prekmurje. All these can be found in variants on the menus of Slovene diplomatic residences.

To show what is going on in our kitchen, I have chosen two menus that reveal the taste of our family and diplomatic colleagues rather than my cooking skills. The first is a typical Slovene Sunday lunch, when the entire family gathers at home, and more cooking is done than usually. This is also close to what is quickly prepared in the residence on Saturdays, when there are no official events; these resipes you will find in the last part of this book.

The second menu (which will follow on the next pages), on the other hand, is an original example of a formal dinner, like the one hosted by the President of the Republic on the occasion of Queen Elizabeth's visit to Slovenia in autumn 2008. In the first menu, the ingredients follow the tradition in my family and some classic Slovene cookbooks. For the second menu, I wanted to keep the proportions and the preparation as they were for the formal dinner, and I am really grateful to the cooks involved in its preparation or their description, provided specifically for this publication; this is their generous contribution to the mission of this book. All recipes serve 4.

One essential element needs to be added: in Slovenia, the wine accompanying food is very important. Not only do the Slovenes produce and drink lots of wine, but on 11 November, we celebrate St Martin's Day, when the must turns into wine and, what is more, our national anthem is a poem by the greatest Slovene poet France Prešeren – 'A Toast' – dedicated to beautiful Slovene girls and to all nations that strive for peace in the world.

I sincerely hope you will enjoy our dishes!

VEGETABLE TRIO: AUBERGINE PARMIGIANA

INGREDIENTS:
2 aubergines
salt
white pepper
olive oil
100 g Nanos cheese
150 g ripe tomatoes
fresh basil

PREPARATION:
Cut aubergines lengthwise and fry the slices in as little oil as possible. Season the fried aubergines with salt and pepper; put a layer of aubergines in an ovenproof dish, followed by a layer of sliced cheese and diced tomato fried on scallions; continue layering. Add at least three layers, finishing with cheese.

Place the ovenproof dish in the oven and bake at 140 °C for 20 minutes.

Allow to cool, cut and serve alone, or in combination with other hors d'oeuvres. Immediately before serving, sprinkle with some cold pressed olive oil.

VEGETABLE TRIO: FILLED ARTICHOKE

INGREDIENTS:
4 artichokes
salt
white pepper
juice of ½ lemon
sugar
olive oil
filling of your choice

PREPARATION:
Peel and core the artichokes; shape into cups and boil in salted water with sugar, olive oil and lemon juice.

Shock the softened artichokes in ice water; correct the shape if necessary – the bottom needs to be flat – and fill, e.g. with crème fraîche, cottage cheese with chives, etc.

VEGETABLE TRIO: BELL PEPPER MOUSSE IN COURGETTE WRAPPING

INGREDIENTS:
1 young courgette (80g)
20 g olive oil
salt
white pepper
fresh dill
juice of ½ lemon
red pepper (100g)
yellow pepper (100g)
100 ml whipping cream
4 g gelatine

PREPARATION:
Slice the courgette, season with salt and pepper, sprinkle with lemon juice and quickly grill on a ribbed grill pan. Sprinkle with olive oil and fresh dill. Allow to cool.

Bell pepper mousse: separately braise each colour of pepper, mash, add whipped cream, fresh spices and salt, bind with gelatine and fill the moulds. Each part of the mould is filled with a different colour.

The cooled mousse is unmoulded, wrapped in a grilled courgette slice, and served.

Accompanying wine: Traminer.

SEA BASS 'PIRAN' WITH CHANTERELLES ON A BUCKWHEAT BED

INGREDIENTS:
4 sea bass fillets (each approx. 200 g)
20 g coarse sea salt
40 g olive oil
400 g chanterelles
80 g onion
50 g butter
0.125 l whipping cream
salt
white pepper
20 g garlic
30 g parsley
60 g buckwheat flour
1 egg
30 g white flour
0.1 litre milk
chives

PREPARATION:
Heat olive oil in a pan and quickly fry the sea bass fillets on both sides. Heat the butter in a saucepan, and add chopped onion and garlic. Stir from time to time and fry until the onion is golden-yellow. Add cleaned chanterelles and fry until the liquid has evaporated. Season the fried chanterelles with salt and freshly ground white pepper.

Add grated lemon zest and whipping cream. Bring to a boil.

The fillets will lie on a buckwheat pastry bed: take buckwheat and white flour, egg, yeast and milk, salt and freshly cut chives to prepare thick whisked dough; bake pastry beds in the form and size of the fillets.

To serve: put each fillet on a buckwheat bed and garnish with chanterelles.

LAMB FILLET WITH ROSEMARY ON CREAM PURÉE WITH GLAZED SHALLOT

INGREDIENTS:
two lamb fillets (back without bones), each approx. 400 g
olive oil
salt
pepper
fresh rosemary
200 g white bread

PREPARATION:
Marinate the lamb fillets. Quickly fry on both sides, garnish one fillet with the bread stuffing (cube the bread, bind with milk and egg, add fried onion, garlic and rosemary), cover with the other fillet, wrap in a fresh pork net.

Bake in the oven at 160–170 °C to an internal meat temperature of 58 °C.

Serve with mashed potatoes enriched with sour cream, and diced vegetables sautéed in butter; the sauce is made of sugar-glazed shallots, soaked in lamb sauce.

Accompanying wine: Pinot Noir.

CHESTNUT TART

INGREDIENTS for the sponge cake:
2 eggs
60 g flour
60 g sugar

Lower filling layer:
125 g chestnut purée
50 g milk chocolate
40 g marrons glacés
125 g whipped cream
rum
vanilla sugar

PREPARATION:
Beat the eggs and sugar, add flour and pour into a spring form pan lined with baking paper; bake.

To prepare the lower filling layer, add tempered milk chocolate, chestnut purée and vanilla sugar to whipped cream. Stir gently and distribute over the cake soaked with sweet rum water. Sprinkle with crushed marrons glacés, cover with another layer of sponge and add the upper filling layer – the vanilla cream: whipped cream with vanilla seeds bound with gelatine.

Garnish with mashed chestnut purée, white chocolate, lemon balm, caramel, etc.

Accompanying wine: Yellow Muscat, berry selection.

SPAIN

Recipes provided by Mrs Elena Meneses de Orozco, spouse of the Spanish Permanent Representative on the North Atlantic Council

Tortilla de Patatas

***

Gazpacho

***

Paella

***

Leche Frita

TORTILLA DE PATATAS (6 SERVINGS)

INGREDIENTS:
8 eggs
1 kg potatoes
2 cups olive oil
salt to taste
optional: one large onion, thinly sliced

PREPARATION:
Peel, wash and dry the potatoes and cut into small pieces about 2 mm thick.

Heat the oil in the frying pan, add potato pieces (and onion pieces) with a little bit of salt.

Cook slowly, on medium heat. Turn occasionally until potatoes are tender, but not brown. They must be loose, not stick together.

Beat eggs in a large bowl with a fork. Salt to taste. Drain potatoes. Add potatoes to beaten eggs, pressing them so that eggs cover them completely. Heat 2 tbsps of the oil in large pan. Add potato-egg mixture, spreading quickly. Lower the heat to medium-high. Shake pan to prevent sticking.

When potatoes start to brown, put a plate on top of the skillet and flip to cook the other side, adding another tbsp of oil.

GAZPACHO (8 SERVINGS)

INGREDIENTS:
1 ¼ peeled mature tomatoes
1/2 medium onion
1 small cucumber (the small chubby Spanish type)
1 small green pepper
optional: some bread from the day before, soaked in water
small portions of diced tomatoes, hard boiled egg, red and green peppers, cucumber, onion to sprinkle on top
1 cup olive oil
2 tbsp of vinegar

PREPARATION:
Put the tomatoes, onion, pepper, cucumber, vinegar, oil and bread into a liquidizer. If you want to dilute it, add a glass of water. Put the mixture into a bowl, add salt and pepper and leave the gazpacho to chill for at least an hour.

If you want to eat it straight away, you can put some ice cubes in to cool it down. Serve the gazpacho in soup bowls, with the portions of diced tomatoes, hard boiled egg, pepper, cucumber on the table, so that everyone can add them to their bowl as they prefer.

PAELLA (8 SERVINGS)

INGREDIENTS:
2/3 glass oil
600 g rice
5 cups fish broth
¼ kg shrimp
1 medium squid
1 kg mussels
¼ kg monkfish
some chorizo, in pieces
1 green pepper
1 red pepper
100 g peas
1 small onion
2 fresh tomatoes
a strand of saffron
garlic
parsley
salt

PREPARATION:
Slice the onions, the tomatoes (better peeled). Put olive oil in a pan, when is warm add these ingredients, then let cook for 5 minutes, put aside.

Meanwhile, in a saucepan, boil the fishbone of the monkfish and the heads of the shrimps. In another pan, boil mussels until they open. Mix the two broths, drain with a colander and set aside.

Heat the paella pan with olive oil, add the green pepper and fried tomatoes and onions. Mix together. When the pepper is tender, add the squid, shrimp and the monkfish. Then add the rice, stirring constantly for a few minutes, then add the broth, distributing it evenly, making sure the rice is covered with liquid. The fire should be fairly high, not interrupting the boil. Crush the garlic, parsley and saffron in a mortar with a little bit of salt. Add two tablespoons of broth. Mix it with the rest of the ingredients. Cook all the ingredients for about 10 minutes over a high fire and taste for salt. Add the shrimp, the mussels, the red paprika and chorizo. Let it cook for another 10 minutes.

It takes about 20 minutes for the paella rice to cook. Do not stir the rice once you have added it to the paella pan, just change its position so that the fire spreads evenly in the pan. All the broth should be absorbed when finished.

Take the paella off the fire and let stand for about 5 minutes, covering it with a kitchen cloth. If the rice has been cooked correctly, the rice grains should be loose, not clumped together or have a mushy texture. Normally, paella is served with some slices of fresh lemon around the paella pan.

Add clams to pan, nestling them into rice mixture. Cook 5 minutes or until shells open; discard any unopened shells. Stir in the seafood mixture and arrange the shrimp, heads down, in the rice mixture. Arrange pimento slices spokelike on top of the rice mixture; cook 5 minutes. Sprinkle with lemon juice. Remove from heat; cover with a towel and let stand 10 minutes.

LECHE FRITA (FRIED MILK, 6 SERVINGS)

INGREDIENTS:
¾ litre milk
5 spoons sugar
25 g butter
2 or 3 eggs
2 egg yolks (optional)
chapelure
1 litre oil
5 tbsp corn flour (maizena)
1 lemon skin
sugar for sprinkling

PREPARATION:
Dilute the flour together with the corn flour and sugar in 1/4l of milk. Boil the rest of the milk with the lemon skin, sugar and butter for ten minutes and add it, after straining, into the prepared paste.

Simmer the mixture on low heat, stirring constantly, for a period of 10 minutes. Put it on a greased tray and allow to cool.

Once the mixture is cold, cut it into squares of about 4 cm, putting them into flour and beaten egg and frying them on medium heat in the olive oil. Dry off the excess oil and sprinkle them with sugar.

You eat them slightly warm.

TURKEY

Recipes contributed by Mrs Arzu Etensel Ildem, spouse of the Turkish Permanent Representative on the North Atlantic Council

Hunkar Begendi
with Egg Plant Purée

***

216

HUNKAR BEGENDI (SULTAN'S DELIGHT, 10 SERVINGS)

INGREDIENTS:
2 kg lamb chunks
4 tbsp butter
3 onions
1 tbsp tomato paste
1 tbsp flour, salt
6 tomatoes
1.5 litre water
1 tsp thyme,
4 cloves garlic
2 bay leaves
½ tsp pepper grains
1 pinch parsley stems

PREPARATION:
Melt the butter in a saucepan. Add the lamb chunks and roast for 8-10 minutes.

Add the sliced onions and the tomato paste, roast for two more minutes and add the flour.

Put the thyme, garlic, bay leaves, pepper grains and parsley in a fine muslin and tie tightly. Add this package to the meat, with salt and water.

Add the tomato chunks to the meat and cook for 10-15 minutes over low heat.

EGGPLANT PURÉE (10 SERVINGS)

INGREDIENTS:
10 eggplants
1 lemon
4 tbsp butter
200 g milk
500 g salt
1 cup gruyère cheese, grated

PREPARATION:
Pierce the eggplants with a fork, place over an open flame or on a high gas flame or on charcoal. Cook for half an hour, turning often until the skin blisters on all slides and the eggplant becomes soft. Once the eggplant has cooled down, cut lengthwise into two.

Scoop out the pulp, squeeze out all the moisture and mash with a fork on a wooden board. Place the eggplant pulp into a bowl and add the lemon juice. Set aside.

Place butter in a saucepan, add flour and cook over low heat, stirring constantly for 2-3 minutes. Add boiled milk and continue stirring for 2-3 minutes. Add salt and pepper. Mix eggplants together with this mixture. Add cheese and mash until it turns into a paste for 1 minute.

Pour the eggplant puree into a serving dish, make a hollow in the centre and arrange the meat in this hollow with a little of its own juice.

UNITED KINGDOM

Recipes provided by Mrs Christine Eldon,
spouse of the Permanent Representative of
the United Kigdom on the North Atlantic Council

Smoked Salmon Paté

***

Lamb with a Herb and Mustard Crust

***

Lemon Surprise Pudding

SMOKED SALMON PATÉ (4 SERVINGS)

INGREDIENTS:
350 g thinly sliced smoked salmon
150 ml double cream
finely grated rind and juice of 1 lemon
salt and ground black pepper
melba toast to serve

PREPARATION:
Line 4 small ramekins with clear plastic wrap. Then line the dishes with 115 g of the smoked salmon cut into strips long enough to flop over the edges.

In a food processor fitted with a metal blade, process the rest of the salmon with the cream, lemon rind and juice, salt and plenty of black pepper.

Pack the lined ramekins with the smoked salmon paté and wrap over the loose strips of salmon. Cover with clear film and chill in the refrigerator for 30 minutes.

Invert on to plates and serve with melba toast.

LAMB WITH A HERB AND MUSTARD CRUST (4 SERVINGS)

INGREDIENTS:
4 boneless loins of lamb, each about 150 g
4 tbsp light olive oil
6 tbsp fresh breadcrumbs
1 tsp chopped thyme
1 tbsp chopped parsley
1 tbsp smooth strong Dijon mustard
1 tbsp wholegrain Dijon mustard
salt and pepper

Sauce:
good brown lamb stock
Pinch of thyme leaves
1 tsp chopped parsley
1 tsp wholegrain Dijon mustard
15 g butter

PREPARATION:
Preheat oven to 200 °C.

Season the lamb with salt and pepper. In a heavy frying pan, heat 3 tbsp of the olive oil until it is nearly smoking. Add the lamb and cook over high heat until well browned all over. This should take about 5 minutes, and the loins should still be rare inside.

Place on a wire rack and allow to cool to room temperature.

Pour the breadcrumbs onto a baking tray and drizzle with the remaining olive oil. Toast in the oven until lightly browned, then allow to cool. Stir in the herbs.

Mix the two mustards together and brush over the top of each loin. Dip the mustard-coated part of the loin into the breadcrumbs and gently press the crumbs on to the mustard.

Set the loins on a baking sheet, crumb side up. Place in the top of the oven and roast for 4-5 minutes for medium rare, or 8 minutes for medium to well done. Remove from the oven and allow to rest in a warm place.

Bring the sauce to the boil and stir in the herbs. Slice each loin into 3 thick slices and serve the sauce separately.

This is nice served with mashed potatoes flavoured with spring onions and a selection of spring vegetables.

LEMON SURPRISE PUDDING (4 SERVINGS)

INGREDIENTS:
4 eggs
110 g butter
275 ml milk
2 lemons
110 g self raising flour
110 g sugar

PREPARATION:
Separate the eggs. Grate the lemon peel and squeeze the juice.

Cream the butter and sugar, add the flour, lemon juice and peel, egg yolks and milk.

Whisk the egg whites separately and fold into the batter mix.

Pour into a deep, buttered 15 cm soufflé dish and bake in a bain marie for 45-50 minutes at 180 °C.

Serve hot, dusted with icing sugar.

UNITED STATES OF AMERICA

Recipes provided by Mrs Karen Volker,
spouse of the Permanent Representative of
the United States on the North Atlantic Council

Cold Cucumber Yogurt Soup

***

Crab Cakes

***

Green Beans and Walnuts

***

Nantucket Cranberry Pie

COLD CUCUMBER YOGURT SOUP

INGREDIENTS:
3 medium cucumbers
4 cloves of garlic
juice of 1 lemon
1 tbsp of olive oil (extra virgin)
1 to 2 tbsp chopped dill
1 pint plain yogurt
1 tbsp chopped mint
1 tsp of sea salt

PREPARATION:
Peel and remove most of the seeds from cucumbers and cut them into chunks. Process all ingredients in a blender or food processor briefly until cucumber is finely chopped. It should retain a slightly crunchy texture. Chill well (at least 2 hours).

This soup may be made a day or 2 ahead. For a nice change, substitute coriander (cilantro) for the chopped dill.

When ready, pour into bowls and garnish with dill (or cilantro, depending on which you choose to use in the soup).

CRAB CAKES - A SOUTHERN DELICACY ... (6 SERVINGS)

INGREDIENTS:
1 lb lump crabmeat (two 2 pound crabs will yield approximately 1 1/4 pound of lump crab meat)
1/4 cup unsalted butter
1/2 small onion, minced (can also use shallots)
1 tbsp of garlic, minced
1 tsp coarse sea salt
2 large eggs
1 tsp of hot paprika
1/2 tsp freshly ground black pepper
2 tbsp prepared tartar sauce
2 slices firm white sandwich bread, torn into small pieces
6 tbsp fresh bread crumbs

PREPARATION:
Pick over the crabmeat to remove any bits of shell and cartilage, being careful not to break up the lumps of crab.

Cook the onion, garlic, and 1/2 of the teaspoon of salt in 1 Tbsp of butter in a small skillet, over medium high heat, until the onion is softened. Let it cool.

Whisk together the eggs, Worcestershire sauce, remaining salt, paprika, pepper, tartar sauce, and onion mixture. Gently fold in the crabmeat and torn bread. Note that the mixture will be very wet. Gently form the mixture into six cakes, each about 3 1/2 inches across and 3/4 inches thick.

Line a tray with a piece of wax paper just large enough to hold the cakes and sprinkle it with half of the bread crumbs.

Set the crab cakes in one layer on the top of the paper and sprinkle with the remaining bread crumbs. Cover the crab cakes loosely with another sheet of wax paper and chill for one hour.

Melt the remaining butter in a large nonstick skillet over medium high heat until the foam subsides. Cook the crab cakes until golden brown, about 3 minutes on each side.

GREEN BEANS AND WALNUTS
(4 SERVINGS)

INGREDIENTS:
green beans, enough for four people
1 cup of walnuts (shelled, broken into small pieces)
2 tbsp of olive oil
1 tbsp of walnut oil
sea salt

PREPARATION:
Trim the green beans so that ends are tidy. Place them in a small amount of boiling water (do not put them in the water until it is already boiling). Boil (steam really as there is not very much water in the pan; certainly not enough to cover the beans) the beans for 5 minutes (no more!). Remove them from the stove quickly and rinse them in cold water to stop the cooking process. Set aside.

While you are prepping the beans, place walnuts in a baking dish and bake them in a warm oven for approximately 20 minutes – do not let them burn! Heat the olive oil and walnut oil (it is important to use the walnut oil as it really helps make the flavor of the walnuts come out) in a frying pan until hot. Add the walnuts and green beans to the pan, stirring over medium heat until the beans are heated again thoroughly. Add salt to taste (perhaps a slight bit more than you would think).

Serve immediately.

NANTUCKET CRANBERRY PIE

INGREDIENTS:
Filling:
2 cups raw cranberries
½ cup sugar
½ cup chopped walnuts

Batter:
2 eggs (beaten)
1 tsp melted butter
¾ cup melted mayonnaise
1 cup flour
1 cup sugar

PREPARATION:
First make the batter by mixing 1 cup of sugar and 1 teaspoon of melted butter and then (when the sugar and butter are mixed) adding the rest of the batter ingredients.

Grease a 10-inch pie plate. Place cranberries on the bottom. Sprinkle ½ cup sugar and nuts over the cranberries.

Cover with batter and bake at 325 °F (about 162 °C) for 35-40 minutes.

This recipe was taken from "The Mount Vernon Cookbook: Virginia Hospitality from the Home of George Washington". (Published by the Mount Vernon Ladies' Association of the Union, Mount Vernon, Virginia).

THIS AND THAT

Most Appreciated, Fast and Easy to Prepare Meals

***

Cookies and Cakes

234

MOST APPRECIATED, FAST AND EASY TO PREPARE MEALS

Fresh Tomato Salad

Beef Soup with Noodles

Sautéed Potaoes, Beef Cooked in Soup and Vegetable Garnish

Seasonal Salad

Nut 'Potica'

Bacon Rolls

Deviled Eggs

Layered Bread Dessert

Butterflied Legs of Lamb with Almonds, Parmesan and Tarragon Crust

Turkey-Hen Goulash with Sherry

Shepherd's Salad

Red Fruit Pudding

FRESH TOMATO SALAD - easy to prepare (4 SERVINGS)

by Karen Volker, United States of America

INGREDIENTS:
assortment of fresh tomatoes – as many kinds and colors as you can find – about 1 ¼ pounds
1 cup basil leaves, cut into julienne strips
basil leaves (whole) for garnish
1 tbsp balsamic vinegar
2 tbsp olive oil (extra virgin)
½ tsp chopped garlic
sea salt and freshly gound black pepper

PREPARATION:
First make the vinaigrette and set it aside: pour the vinegar and salt into a small bowl, add the olive oil, garlic, and pepper and mix. Adjust seasonings to taste.

Wash and slice the large tomatoes, quarter the medium ones, and halve the small ones. Leave the current tomatoes (if you've included any) whole. Toss with balsamic vinaigrette and the julienned basil leaves. To assembly, divide the tomatoes among 4 luncheon plates and garnish them with whole basil leaves.

This recipe was taken from "Cooking with Nora", by Nora Pouillon, the owner and chef at Restaurant NORA in Washington, D.C.

BEEF SOUP WITH NOODLES - dish 1 of a traditional Slovene lunch

by Martina Skok, Slovenia

INGREDIENTS:
Soup:
1kg good quality beef
some marrow bones
2 l water
1 parsley root
3 carrots
leek, celery, onion, salt, pepper

Noodles:
1 egg
120 g flour

PREPARATION:
Put the soup ingredients into a pot, cover with cold water, bring to the boil, and simmer slowly for 1 hour. Before serving, sieve the soup (keep the meat and vegetables for the main dish). Cook noodles in a little water. The soup is served clear; guests add the cooked noodles to their taste from a separate bowl.

Noodles can be prepared a day or two in advance. Make dough from flour and egg. Divide the dough into smaller lumps and roll thinly. Leave to dry on a cotton cloth. Cut the rolled dough into several equal bands, stack one on the top of the other or fold into a roll, and cut as thinly as possible. Spread the noodles over a cloth and leave briefly to dry; you can then store them for several days.

SAUTÉED POTATOES, BEEF COOKED IN SOUP AND VEGETABLE GARNISH - dish 2 of a traditional Slovene lunch

by Martina Skok, Slovenia

INGREDIENTS:
1 kg potatoes
2 tbsp of fat
1 onion
salt, pepper
1 ladle of soup (if necessary)
meat and vegetables from the soup

PREPARATION:
Cook potatoes in slightly salted water, peel and cut into slices; put into a frying pan with oil or lard and onion, and stir fry slowly. Stir from time to time with a wooden spoon or fork, mash well, and leave to fry until a crust forms.

Turn over and leave to fry on the other side. Repeat several times, mixing the crust into the mass so that the potatoes go slightly brown. The potatoes may be garnished with scratchings, various sauces (tomato, vegetable, etc.) or mayonnaise.

Serve with the meat and vegetables cooked in the soup.

SEASONAL SALAD - dish 3 of a traditional Slovene lunch & fast to prepare

by Martina Skok, Slovenia

In the summer, we prepare tomato salad with onions, and in the winter, chicory with beans, garlic and eggs. Season with wine or apple vinegar, and olive, pumpkin or sunflower oil.

Accompanying wine: my recommendation is Refošk or Chardonnay.

NUT 'POTICA' - dish 4 of a traditional Slovene lunch

by Martina Skok, Slovenia

INGREDIENTS:
Yeast mixture:
4 tbsp milk
1 tbsp sugar
30 g yeast
100 g flour

Dough:
0.75 litre milk
100 g sugar
120 g unsalted butter
salt
1kg flour
2 egg yolks
30 g grease

Filling:
1–2 eggs
grated zest of ½ lemon
0.5 kg ground walnuts
0.25 kg sugar
vanilla sugar, rum, cinnamon

PREPARATION:
Put lukewarm milk, 1 tablespoon of sugar, flour and yeast into a cup. Mix the ingredients and allow to rise.

In a large bowl, mix warm milk, sugar, butter, 1 level teaspoon of salt, egg yolks and flour. Mix and add the yeast and grease. Mix together and knead until the mass becomes smooth and fluffy. Sprinkle the dough with flour and leave in a warm place to rise.

While the dough is rising, scald the nuts with boiling milk; add eggs, sugar and spices.

After the dough has risen to approximately double size, roll it, spread the filling, and roll it up. Fold the roll and put it into a greased
and floured cake tin.

Cover and leave to rise in a warm place for another 30 minutes. Brush with whisked egg, put into a preheated oven and bake on medium heat for about 1 hour.

This makes two medium-sized potica rolls that can be cut into a number of portions.

Potica can be kept for several days in an airtight container and at room temperature.

Potica is served with coffee.

BACON ROLLS (PIRAGI) - favourite Latvian very traditional recipe

by Brigita Eichmane, Latvia

Piragi (bacon rolls) filled with diced fatty bacon and onion are still baked today for almost all Latvian celebrations. Various sweet platter breads are also baked, which are topped with rhubarb, apples, berries in summer and sweetened cottage cheese or dried apples in autumn.

INGREDIENTS:
450-500 g flour
250 ml milk or water
25 g yeast,
75 g margarine or butter
25 g sugar
5 g salt
1 egg

Filling:
350 g smoked streaky bacon
50 g onion
ground pepper

PREPARATION:
Prepare dough (see below). After dough has risen, divide into 30-35 g pieces, roll into round balls and leave on a pastry board for 10-15 minutes to rise. Press each piece flat, place bacon filling in the centre, press together edges of dough above or at the side of the filling. Roll with both hands to even out filling; make the shape

long with slender ends and bent into a half-moon. Place on a greased baking tray, leave to rise, brush with beaten egg and bake in a hot oven.

Brush with melted butter once removed from the oven.

Bacon filling: Cut rind off bacon. Dice bacon and onion and sauté (sauté only for a short period, so that fat does not run off), add pepper and mix well.

Yeast Dough for Piragi (bacon rolls) and sweet breads:
Sift flour. Mix yeast with warm water and flour and put in a warm place to rise for 15-20 minutes. Dissolve salt and sugar in water or milk which has been heated to 30-35 °C, add beaten eggs, yeast, sifted flour (leave approximately 5-6 % of flour for kneading and shaping) and stir to form an even dough. Add melted butter and knead, until the dough springs back from your hands and edges of the bowl. Pat down the dough, sprinkle with flour.

Cover the bowl with a lid or clean cloth and put in a warm place to rise. After 1 hour the dough will have nearly doubled in size. Punch down dough to release carbon dioxide and continue to rise for 1 hour. Best results will be achieved if the temperature of the dough is 25-30 °C.

DEVILED EGGS - favourite Latvian very traditional recipe

by Brigita Eichmane, Latvia

INGREDIENTS:
4 eggs
2 tbsp butter (room temperature)
2 tbsp mayonnaise
1/2 tsp mustard
salt
pepper

For garnish: fresh herbs, cranberries or anchovies

PREPARATION:
Boil the eggs for 10 minutes. Run cold water over the eggs and let them cool in the water for 10 minutes. Peel off the eggshell. Halve the eggs and remove the yolks. With a wooden spoon press the yolks through a sieve. Add to the yolks the butter, mayonnaise and mustard. Use the spoon to mash them all together into a paste. Season with salt and pepper.

Using a pastry tube return the yolks to the egg whites.

Garnish with cranberries and herbs.

LAYERED BREAD DESSERT (RUPJMAIZES KARTOJUMS) - favourite Latvian very traditional recipe & easy to prepare

by Brigita Eichmane, Latvia

INGREDIENTS:
75 g dry rye bread
50 g loganberry jam
20 g sugar
60 g whipping cream
cinnamon
vanilla essence

PREPARATION:
Finely grate rye bread, mix with cinnamon and half of the sugar. Beat cream, adding sugar and vanilla essence gradually, until mixture forms stiff peaks.

On a shallow dish, arrange layers of bread, jam and whipped cream, finishing with a layer of bread which is decorated with whipped cream.

BUTTERFLIED LEG OF LAMB WITH ALMONDS, PARMESAN AND TARRAGON CRUST - most appreciated

by Hólmfridur Kofoed-Hansen, Iceland

INGREDIENTS:
1 butterflied leg of lamb
1/2 cup chopped almonds
1/2 cup grated parmesan cheese
1/2 cup breadcrumbs
1/2 cup chopped fresh tarragone leaves
1/2 cup of extra virgin olive oil
juice of 1 lemon
salt and pepper from the mill

PREPARATION:
Blend everything well together.

Sear the butterflied open boneless leg of lamb on both sides on a hot frying pan or a grill. Salt and pepper to taste.

Preheat oven to 270 °F.

Put the seared lamb with skin side down on an ovenproof dish with a grill. Roast in the oven for about 12-15 minutes. Take out of the oven and spread the almond-parmesan-tarragone mix evenly over the roast of lamb.

Roast it further for about 12-15 minutes until the crust is golden brown.

TURKEY-HEN GOULASH WITH SHERRY - most appreciated

by Hana Füleová, Czech Republic

INGREDIENTS:
750 g turkey-hen meat cut into small cubes
2 tbsp oil or fat
1 large onion, diced
1 clove of garlic, crushed
2 carrots, cut into slices
salt, black pepper
cayenne pepper
1/2 tsp dried thyme
1/4 tsp dried marjoram
100 ml dry sherry
250 ml chicken broth
1 tsp Maizena (cornstarch)
3 tbsp sour cream
fresh parsley tops, chopped

PREPARATION:
Heat oil in a heavy skillet. Add meat and brown for 2-3 minutes. Add onion, garlic and carrots. Stir and cook for another 3 minutes. Add spices and half of the sherry and chicken broth. Cover and simmer over low heat for 25 minutes.

Mix rest of chicken broth and sherry with Maizena. Add mixture and cook for 1 minute. Add sour cream. Add parsley.

Serve over rice.

SHEPHERD'S SALAD - most appreciated

by Maryana Ivanova, Bulgaria

INGREDIENTS:
tomatoes
cucumbers
fresh peppers
fresh onions
field mushrooms
1 boiled egg
yellow cheese
ham
parsley
vegetable oil, vinegar, salt, black pepper

PREPARATION:
Wash and clean well the tomatoes, the cucumbers, the fresh peppers and the fresh onion. Peel the cucumbers. Cut all vegetables into big cubes. Clean and peel the mushrooms and cut them into circles. Cut the yellow cheese and the ham into smaller cubes than the vegetable cubes. Wash the parsley and cut it into small pieces.

Put all the products prepared in the above manner in a deep bowl. Add the oil, the vinegar, the salt and the black pepper (first grind the black pepper well) and stir. Cut the hard boiled egg into thin slices.
Transfer the salad you have prepared into a soup-plate and garnish it with the thin slices of hard boiled egg.

RED FRUIT PUDDING - most appreciated in summer

by Barbara Brandenburg, Germany

INGREDIENTS:
250 g blackberries, red currants, raspberries and strawberries each (weighed after being prepared)
35 g cornflour (cornstarch)
100 g sugar
500 ml fruit juice (e.g. cherry or red currant juice)

PREPARATION:
Sort the blackberries, wash carefully and drain thoroughly. Wash the red currants, drain well and remove from the stalks. Sort the raspberries but do not wash. Wash the strawberries, drain, remove the stalks and cut into halves or quarters, depending on size.

Mix the cornflour with the sugar, add 4 tbsp of the juice and stir well. Bring the rest of the juice to the boil in a saucepan. Stir in the cornflour mixture, bring to the boil and remove the saucepan from the heat. Add the fruit and stir well. Put the fruit pudding in a glass bowl or in pudding bowls and refrigerate.

Serve with vanilla sauce or whipping cream. Delicious also with semolina pudding (recipe in the German section of this book).

COOKIES AND CAKES

Shortbread

***

Scones

***

German Cheese Cake

***

Frankfurter Kranz

SHORTBREAD - most appreciated (makes 6-8 wedges)

by Christine Eldon, United Kingdom

INGREDIENTS:
115 g unsalted butter
50 g caster sugar
115 g plain flour
50 g rice flour or semolina

PREPARATION:
Preheat oven to 160 °C.

Beat the butter and sugar together until light and fluffy. Stir in the plain flour and rice flour or semolina, then knead lightly until smooth.

Press the dough evenly into a 15cm loose bottomed flan ring, pinching the edges with your thumb and forefinger to make a crimped edge. Prick the surface with a fork and then mark into 6 or 8 wedges.

Bake the shortbread for about 40 minutes until pale biscuit coloured and just firm to the touch.

Leave the shortbread to cool for a few minutes then gently transfer to a wire rack to cool completely.

To serve, break the shortbread along the marked lines and dust with icing sugar.

SCONES - most appreciated (10-12 SERVINGS)

by Christine Eldon, United Kingdom

INGREDIENTS:
225 g self raising flour or 225 g plain flour plus ½ tsp bicarbonate of soda and 1 teaspoon cream of tartar
40 g butter at room temperature
1 ½ tbsp caster sugar
pinch of salt
150 ml milk
a little extra flour

PREPARATION:
Preheat the oven to 220 °C.
Sift the flour into a bowl and rub the butter into it rapidly, using your fingertips. Stir in the sugar and salt, then take a knife and use it to mix in the milk little by little.
Flour your hands lightly and knead the mixture to a soft dough, adding a drop more milk if it feels too dry. Turn the dough out onto a floured pastry board and roll it out to a thickness of about 2 cm using a lightly floured rolling pin. Take a 4 or 5cm pastry cutter and place it on the dough and tap it down sharply to cut it neatly. Cut as many shapes as you can, kneading the dough trimmings together until you have used it all.

Place the scones on an ungreased baking tray and brush them with a little extra milk. Bake near the top of the oven for 12-15 minutes until well risen and golden. Cool on a wire rack and eat them while warm, with butter or whipped cream and jam.

GERMAN CHEESE CAKE - my absolute favourite cake!

by Barbara Brandenburg, Germany

INGREDIENTS:
For the shortcrust pastry:
150 g plain (all-purpose) flour
½ level tsp baking powder
75 g sugar
3 drops vanilla essence in a tbsp sugar
1 pinch salt
1 medium egg
75 g soft butter or margarine

For the filling:
whites of 3 medium eggs
250 ml chilled whipping cream
750 g low fat curd cheese
150 g sugar
2 tbsp lemon juice
50 g (6 tbsp) cornflour (cornstarch)
yolks of 3 medium eggs

PREPARATION:
Preheat the oven (about 200 °C) and grease the base of the springform tin.

To make the dough, mix together the flour and baking powder, sift into a mixing bowl and add the other ingredients. Stir with a hand mixer with a kneading hook until the dough is formed. Then roll it into a ball using your hands. Roll out two-thirds of the dough, line the greased base of the springform tin with it and put the ring back around the base. Prick the base several times, put the mould on a baking tray in the oven and pre-bake the cake for about 10 minutes.

After removing from the oven put the springform tin on a rack and let the cheesecake base cool down a little. Roll the rest of the dough into a long cylinder and place around the base, pressing lightly against the sides to form an edge 3 cm high.

To make the filling, first beat the egg whites until they are very stiff, then whip the cream until stiff. Mix together the curd cheese, sugar, lemon juice, cornflour and egg yolks. Now fold the stiffly beaten egg whites and whipped cream into the cream cheese mixture and spread this mixture evenly over the cheesecake base. Put the springform tin back into the oven (160 °C) for about 60-70 minutes.

When done, turn off the oven but leave the cheesecake inside with the door slightly open for another 15 minutes to prevent the top from cracking. Then put the cheesecake on a rack to cool down but without removing it from the mould.

FRANKFURTER KRANZ - of which I have fond childhood memories: a little bit difficult, but worth a try (we had it only on birthdays)

by Barbara Brandenburg, Germany

INGREDIENTS:
For the cake mixture:
100 g soft margarine or butter
150 g sugar
2-3 drops vanilla essence in a tbsp sugar
4 drops lemon essence
1 pinch salt
3 medium eggs
150 g plain (all-purpose) flour
50 g cornflour (cornstarch)
2 level tsp baking powder

For the praline:
10 g (2 tsp) butter
60 g sugar
125 g blanched almonds, chopped

For the cream:
40 g (4.5 tsp) custard powder, vanilla flavour
100 g sugar
500 ml milk
250 g soft butter

In addition:
2 tbsp red currant jelly or strawberry jam
some candied cherries
Guggelhupf or ring mould, 22 cm

PREPARATION:
Preheat the oven top and bottom (180 °C). Grease the ring mould.

To make the cake mixture, stir the softened margarine or butter with a hand mixer with whisk until it becomes smooth. Gradually add the sugar, vanilla sugar, flavouring and salt. Stir until the mixture thickens. Add 1 egg at a time, whisking each one for about ½ minute at the highest setting. Mix together the flour and baking powder, sift and stir briefly into the butter and egg mixture into the ring mould, smooth out the surface and put on a baking tray in the oven for about 40 minutes.

Leave the cake in the mould for 10 minutes after taking it out of the oven, then remove from the tin and leave to cool. To make the praline, stir together the butter, sugar and almonds over low heat until the mixture turns brown, pour onto a piece of aluminium foil and leave to cool.

To make the butter cream, make the custard following the instructions on the package, but with 100 g sugar and 500 ml milk. Let the custard cool (do not refrigerate), stir occasionally. Whisk the softened butter with a hand mixer until smooth and stir into the cooled custard a spoonful at a time, making sure that butter and custard are both at room temperature, or else it may curdle.

Whisk the jelly until it is smooth or rub the jam through a sieve. Cut the ring cake horizontally twice to make three layers and spread the jam or jelly on the bottom layer. Spread half the butter cream on the 2 lower layers, then put the top layer in place, thus reassembling the ring cake. Now coat the ring cake with the remaining butter cream (reserving 1-2 tbsp) and sprinkle the praline all over the cake.

Put the reserved cream in a piping bag with a star-shaped nozzle and decorate the cake. Finally, garnish with candied cherries and refrigerate for about 2 hours.

LAST BUT NOT LEAST

THE BEST HOSTS ARE ALSO THE BEST GUESTS

by Martina Skok, Slovenia

All the events I host are very dear to me. I consider every event something special, and meeting people that my husband and I invite to our residence is always a welcome opportunity to make new friendships, learn about unknown worlds, hear new stories from the past, and possibly establish new relations for the future. From this point of view, there are no 'awful' dinners or lunches or events that are significantly more or less pleasant than others. All of them are agreeable; it is just that some could also be a little more relaxed.

There are many elements in the scenario of an event that may make the host feel disconcented. To me, the most stressful thing is to be forced to change the cook or the caterer – one is not sure about the quality of food, the professionalism or the skill of waiters, etc. Another rather stressful situation may arise when the host is not familiar with the venue: dinners with a large number of guests are often organized outside the residence, and it may happen that you don't know the restaurant or the dining area, or that you are not aware of possible other simultaneous events that may be taking place there. Furthermore, your guests may have questions that you are not able to answer, and so on. It is also very important to learn in advance the names of your guests – and to bear in mind why you have invited them at all.

For all these reasons, I prefer to host dinners and lunches at the residence. I feel more self-confident and relaxed. I know where to sit, how long it will take for the waiter to come back from the kitchen if he or she forgot something, how loud I have to speak if I want everybody to hear me, etc. Our residence is small, and normally we can only host up to twelve people around the table. In fact, I prefer it that way, as otherwise it is difficult to really get to know all the guests and to talk to them properly. Already in Ancient Rome, feasts were organized with only nine people around a table; as far as I'm concerned, that would do just fine for today's purposes.

Nevertheless, even at home, things can go better or worse. From my first ladies luncheon, which I hosted at the time of my husband's first ambassadorial post in Canada in spring 1998, and still remember rather well, I recall that I kept the ladies sitting around the table for an unusually long time after lunch. In fact, I thought that coffee would first be brought to the salon and then we would all move there from the dining room; of course, just the opposite would have been right. No one said a word: we were just sitting and sitting and talking and talking, until the waiter eventually asked me directly if I wanted coffee to be served at the table. Only then did we move into the salon.

From another, very recent dinner, I remember the cook arriving at the residence very late, only minutes before the arrival of the guests. We called him 45 minutes before the dinner to be sure that he was on his way, but he was still on the other side of town.

Luckily, the food was easy to finalize, and we also had to wait for one of the guests who could not find our residence for quite some time; in the end, this probably saved the dinner.

There are many other interesting memories about dinners. Once the caterer wanted to serve food on specially designed plates, but it turned out that, when they were brought to the table, they did not fit the underplates and were standing in a very funny position. On other occasions the caterer forgot to bring the bread, the butter or the ice and then had to drive to the local corner shop to get the necessary items at the last moment. We even had to host some events in a residence that was not yet completely furnished and decorated.

The good thing in such circumstances is that most people you invite understand the situation very well. Usually, they have all gone through similar situations before and are very well aware of what may happen at such events. Like the host, they prefer to look on the bright side. Indeed, the best hosts are also the best guests. They know what it means if somebody reaches out to them with a proposal for an agreeable event, even if that may mean being offered food that is not their favourite or sitting next to somebody who speaks only languages they don't understand, and so on.

Be that as it may, such moments are all the more precious if only one thinks how lucky we are just to sit at those beautifully arranged tables with candles and flowers, colourful and tasty food and gold and red wine... Hospitality, cuisine and conversations over meals are arts, and I am profoundly honoured and grateful for all those marvellous art works that I have enjoyed as the spouse of an ambassador to NATO.

INDEX IN ALPHABETICAL ORDER

Amaretto ice cream (p. 124)
Anytime soup (p. 13)
Apples under the blankets (p. 157)
Appeltjes onder de deken (p. 157)
Apples in blankets (p. 57)
Aubergine parmigiana (p. 199)

Bacalhau Espiritual (p. 177)
Bacon rolls (p. 243)
Baked apples (p. 147)
Baked ham with maple glaze (p. 42)
Beef olives (p. 87)
Beef soup with liver dumplings (p. 52)
Beef soup with noodles (p. 238)
Beef with cream sauce (p. 53)
Bell pepper mousse in courgette wrapping (p. 201)
Boiled veal (p. 33)
Braised leg of lamb with white wine, sage, tomatoes and mushrooms (p. 115)
Breaded cheese peppers (p. 35)
Bryndza dumplings (p. 189)
Bryndzove halusky (p. 189)
Butterflied leg of lamb with almonds, parmesan and tarragon crust (p. 247)

Cabbage wraps with meat or vegetable filling (p. 145)
Chestnut tart (p. 205)
Chicken "Thrace" (p. 37)

Chicken jelly (p. 143)
Chocolate mousse (p. 29)
Cod fish (p. 177)
Cold cucumber soup with fresh mint (p. 168)
Cold cucumber yogurt soup (p. 227)
Consommé with Tokay wine (p. 105)
Cooked cream and fresh berries (p. 131)
Crab cakes (p. 228)
Cream of white asparagus soup (p. 25)
Crevettes à l'ail (p. 77)
Croatian stuffed calamari (p. 47)
Cured salmon (p. 161)
Czech raised dumplings (p. 55)

Deviled eggs (p. 245)

Eggplant purée (p. 218)
Eggs in aspic 'Munkácsy style' (p. 103)

Filled artichoke (p. 200)
Fillet of beef 'Budapest style' (p. 106)
Frankfurter Kranz (p. 257)
Fresh salmon tartar on potato pancakes (p. 167)
Fresh tomato salad (p. 237)

Garides me feta (p. 93)
Gazpacho (p. 210)
Gehaktballen (p. 156)

German cheese cake (p. 255)
Gooseberry mousse with whipping cream (p. 139)
Green beans and walnuts (p. 230)
Grilled Baltic herring on a bed of salad (p. 69)

Ham rolls with horseradish whipped cream (p. 51)
Honey cake (p. 22)
Hunkar begendi (p. 217)
Hvidore grilled scallops (p. 61)

Kettle goulash (p. 191)
Koninginnesoep (p. 155)
Kotlikovy gulás (p. 191)

Lamb fillet with rosemary on cream purée with glazed shallot (p. 204)
Lamb meat with yoghurt (p. 21)
Lamb roulade with purée of parsnip and three sauces of peppers (p. 184)
Lamb with a herb and mustard crust (p. 222)
Layered bread dessert (p. 246)
Leche frita (p. 213)
Lemon surprise pudding (p. 224)
Limoncello (p. 132)
Lobster salad (p. 41)

Meatballs (p. 156)
Milk pie (p. 38)

Minced pork wrapped in cabbage leaves (p. 70)
Mustard sauce (p. 163)
Nantucket cranberry pie (p. 231)
Norwegian gravlaks (p. 161)
Nut 'Potica' (p. 241)

Old German potato soup (p. 85)
Orange roll (p. 179)
Orat al forno with insalata mista (p. 129)

Paella (p. 211)
Panfried fillet of arctic char on fennel, tomato and orange (p. 113)
Panna cotta con mirtilli (p. 131)
Papanasi with cheese and sour cream (p. 185)
Peas with dill and fresh onions (p. 96)
Pickled carp with polenta (p. 183)
Pirohy (p. 193)
Plum tart with currant jelly (p. 151)
Potato dumplings with plum and orange jam (p. 171)
Prawn soup (p. 175)
Preserved lemons (p. 80)

Queen's soup (p. 155)
Quetsche tort (p. 151)

Raspberry charlotte with raspberry sauce (p. 72)
Ravani (p. 98)
Red fruit pudding (p. 250)

Red Salad (p. 144)
Rivica (p. 47)
Roast lamb (p. 95)
Roast pork with rye bread and bacon cubes (p. 137)
Roast potatoes, baked in olive oil and herbs (p. 97)
Rolled wild boar fillet with forest mushroom sauce (p. 169)
Rupjmaizes kartojums (p. 246)

Salade d'oranges et tuiles aux amandes (p. 81)
Sautéed potatoes, beef cooked in soup and vegetable garnish (p. 239)
Scones (p. 254)
Sea bass 'Piran' with chanterelles on a buckwheat bed (p. 202)
Sea bass in the oven (p. 129)
Seasonal salad (p. 240)
Semolina pudding (p. 89)
Semifreddo di amaretti (p. 124)
Shepard's salad (p. 249)
Shortbread (p. 253)
Shrimp baked with feta (p. 93)
Skyr soufflé ice cream (p. 117)
Smoked salmon paté (p. 221)
Spinach pies (p. 20)
Sponge cake 'Somló style' (p. 108)
Stewed potatoes (p. 164)
Sugar pie with whipped cream (p. 43)
Summer lasagna (p. 122)
Summery apple parfait with caramel sauce (p. 64)

Tajine d'agneau aux citrons confits (p. 78)
The Empress' New Year cod (p. 62)
Tortilla de patatas (p. 209)
Trenette al pesto (p. 127)
Trout cakes with chive and lemon sauce (p. 135)
Turkey-hen goulash with sherry (p. 248)

Vegetable trio (p. 199)
Vitello tonnato (p. 121)

Waterzooi of fish (p. 27)

MEASURES

1 kg = 2 1/4 lb
100 g = 3.5 oz
1 oz = 25 g
1 lb = 445 g

1 litre = 1 3/4 pints = 4 1/2 cups
1 cl = 10 ml
1 dl = 100 ml

120 °C = 250 °F
140 °C = 285 °F
160 °C = 325 °F
180 °C = 350 °F
200 °C = 400 °F
220 °C = 425 °F
250 °C = 500 °F

ABBREVIATIONS

tbsp = tablespoon
tsp = teaspoon
g = gram
kg = kilogram
ml = millilitre
l = litre
lb = pound
oz = ounce
fl oz = fluid ounce
°C = degrees Celsius
°F = degrees Fahrenheit